Beach

Kaneohe Bay

Kealakekua Bay

The Art of the Aloha Shirt
by Brown & Arthur

The Art of the Aloha Shirt

DeSoto Brown & Linda Arthur

ISLAND HERITAGE

Attention, shoppers: At Hilo Sales & Surplus in 1952, rayon aloha shirts were bargains at $1.69 or $2.39 (two for $4.50.) (Roger Coryell, Bishop Museum)

Published by Island Heritage Publishing

ISBN 0-89610-405-2

Address orders and correspondence to:

 ISLAND HERITAGE
PUBLISHING

94-411 Kō'aki Street

Waipahu, Hawai'i 96797

For Order: 1-800-468-2800 For Information: (808)-564-8800

Fax 808-564-8888

www.islandheritage.com

Designed by Danvers Fletcher

Printed in Hong Kong

First edition, first printing, 2002

INTRODUCTION

Let Hawaii Dress You Right

What is an aloha shirt? Is it simply a shirt manufactured, or worn, in Hawai'i? Or is it a shirt made of cloth that has a certain pattern? Perhaps the real definition, as with so many other things, is just that we know an aloha shirt when we see one.

So with that simple thought in mind, instead of trying to explain what an aloha shirt is, we should examine where it came from and how it evolved. That story primarily took place in the 20th century, but has its beginnings far earlier, in the many forces that affected Hawai'i and its variety of people—it was out of the dynamics of the people that the shirt came to be.

Hawai'i is known for its remarkable ethnic mix, and, seen historically, the process of racial blending occurred in a relatively short period. When the 1800s began, the islands' population was composed almost entirely of Hawaiians. However, with the increasing influx of Europeans and Americans and their diseases, the Hawaiian population was decimated in the first few decades of the century. Later, as large-scale agriculture developed, too few Hawaiians abandoned their traditional lifestyles to meet the need for plantation workers, so people were brought in from other countries. Generally speaking, Chinese immigration began in the 1850s, followed by the Portuguese in the late 1870s, Japanese in the late 1880s, and Koreans and Filipinos after 1900. Subsequent intermarriage between these many groups led to the extraordinary diversity now seen in Hawai'i; today, more than one-third of all marriages are interracial.

On the cover of the 1965 American Automobile Association's Hawai'i guidebook, Mr. Average Tourist (in his new aloha shirt) appreciates a Waikiki hula show.

A Hawai'i Visitors Bureau brochure from the mid-1950s urges tourists to buy island-made clothing (above).

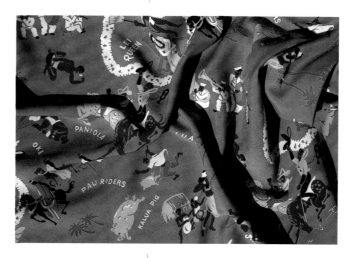

People in Hawai'i often choose to identify themselves in two ways, both as members of a particular ethnic group and as "local." Despite the passage of time and the effects of acculturation (the adaptations made by cultures exposed to new influences), many people retain aspects of their original ethnic heritage, participating in festivals and events, eating certain foods, speaking native languages, and observing various religions. But, especially for the many people with multiple ethnic backgrounds, the larger identification of being "local"—that is, being from Hawai'i, regardless of race—is important. The proud expression of this localness can range from speaking pidgin to wearing Hawai'i's aloha attire.

In a way, the aloha shirt is a unifying symbol of the aloha spirit, a major theme in Hawai'i representing goodwill within a diverse community. Hawaiian textiles in general, and the aloha shirt in particular, have become visible manifestations of Hawai'i's multicultural population.

The "classic" rayon alohawear worn by all these happy party-goers reached its height of popularity in the early 1950s. Today, any one of these garments in top condition would sell on the collectors' market for prices no one back then could possibly have imagined.

Girls dressed in a rainbow of Hawaiian patterns brighten this 1953 magazine cover (Courtesy PacificBasin Communications).

ROOTS OF THE ALOHA SHIRT

The roots of the aloha shirt—and by extension, the entire alohawear industry in Hawai'i—are diverse. Influences of Hawai'i's many racial groups are found in both the cut of clothing and, more significantly, in the motifs used for fabric designs. Some of these elements are easy to identify while others are less apparent, and aren't as well known.

Before Westerners arrived, the Hawaiian people were clad in various garments made of kapa, a fabric found throughout the Pacific. Girls and women (whose main occupation kapa-making was) labored through the lengthy and physically demanding process of stripping, pounding, and dyeing the bark of the wauke (mulberry) to make it into kapa. After much work, the end result was a fine, soft fabric that was not only worn as a garment but was also used almost as a currency to pay a form of taxes that ali'i (royalty) could demand from the common people.

While variations of kapa were produced in many widely-scattered Pacific cultures, many later researchers believed that Hawaiian women reached the highest level of expertise. Surviving kapa shows the wide range of beautiful colors (made from various natural dyes) and unique patterns (pressed onto the fabric by carved wood stencils) that Hawai'i's artisans once produced.

This flourishing tradition, which nearly every Hawaiian woman probably engaged in, died out completely in the span of approximately one hundred years after Westerners arrived in Hawai'i in the late 1700s. Among the factors that contributed to its death: the switch to a currency-based economy in which kapa could no longer be

Sheltered by a banana leaf, a Tahitian couple of the late 1800s shows how the pareu was worn by both men and women - in this case, over western-style clothing (Bishop Museum).

Local manufacturer Alfred Shaheen first sold its popular "Antique Tapa" print in 1951. The pattern incorporated motifs found on original Hawaiian kapa in the Bishop Museum collection (Camille Shaheen-Tunberg).

used to pay taxes; the introduction of durable and colorful machine-made fabrics that didn't fall apart when they got wet; and the desire of many women to free themselves of the unending labor kapa-making required. Like so many aspects of traditional Hawaiian culture, kapa production in Hawai'i faded away until its painstaking revival in the late 20th century.

So what has this to do with aloha shirts? Actually, very little. There was no overlap period when both existed concurrently; Hawaiian kapa had been out of active production for decades by the time the first aloha shirts were being created. Even the original Hawaiian patterns were little noted by 20th century fabric designers, mainly because actual kapa was so rare. The so-called "tapa" patterns popular in the 1950s—assumed by most people at the time to be the epitome of Hawaiian tradition—were, in fact, copies of Samoan material (called tapa). Although of similar fabrication, the latter's design had little in common with authentic Hawaiian designs in either color or pattern. The misattribution occurred because Samoan tapa was still being made and exported to Hawai'i specifically for sale as souvenir items, while Hawaiian kapa was only found in museums and a few private collections.

Design elements copied from the traditional fabrics of different Pacific cultures appear on these shirts (University of Hawai'i's CTAHR Historic Costume Collection).

11

Distinctive pareu patterns were commonly referred to as "Tahitian" in the 1950s and '60s, as in this 1959 advertisement.

One of the earliest such fabric patterns was created in 1939 by graphic artist John MacMillan (later known as John Meigs, or professionally as Keoni.) In consultation with Edwin Bryan of the Bishop Museum, he studied tapa pieces in the museum's collections and did two separate designs, one incorporating Samoan motifs and the other Hawaiian. When the new fabrics were completed, the museum displayed MacMillan's prints alongside the original pieces he'd been inspired by.

The wearing of Western-style clothing in Hawai'i began soon after outside people began to visit. Captain James Cook and his ships were the first to make contact in 1778, and as explorers like him continued to come, so too, did ships bearing people from military men to entrepreneurs to Christian missionaries. The ali'i first adapted the fashions and objects of the outsiders, but foreign clothing, especially, soon spread to all. The growth of Western religion in particular, which associated bare skin with the sins of sexual desire, spurred Hawaiians to cover themselves more thoroughly than their previous

Nearly all pareu prints consisted of a white design on a solid background. Occasionally, as shown in the photo on the left in this 1957 ad, two colors might be used - but purists might object to tampering with traditions this way.

garments ever had. Women came to universally be covered in the enveloping mu'umu'u, even for swimming. By the time photography became widespread in Hawai'i, in about the 1870s, virtually no Hawaiians were still wearing anything made of kapa. While men continued to wear a malo (loincloth) for swimming or field work, it was made of imported cotton fabric. (It's worth noting also that no woman at the time walked around bare-breasted; any such historic photos are evidence of the photographer's persuasive abilities, not real life.)

As Hawaiians gradually shifted to Western clothing, so did many other Pacific island peoples as they too, came under the influence (and eventual outright control) of outsiders. A clothing style from Tahiti, the pareu, would have some influence on the development of Hawai'i's garment industry. The pareu was nothing more than a simple piece of cotton cloth, manufactured and printed in Europe. By the middle to late 1800s, the pareu came to be universally worn by both sexes in Tahiti; it could be worn by itself or combined with other pieces of clothing. The most notable aspect of the pareu was its bold and simple designs of various semi-abstract motifs (often floral, but not always), most commonly in white on a plain, solid background color. The vision of a Polynesian woman wrapped in a clinging pareu became something of a cliche of the exotic South Seas to

DOROTHY LAMOUR and **JON**

ALOMA OF THE SOUTH SEAS

with LYNNE OVERMAN · PHILIP REED · KATHERINE de MILLE · FRITZ LEIBER · DONA DRAKE · DIRECTED B'
A PARAM

Screen Play by Frank Butler, Seena Owen and Lillie Hayward   Story by Seena Owen and Kurt Siodmak   From the Play by LeRoy Clemens and John B Hymer

many Americans by the 20th century. When Dorothy Lamour appeared in a series of "jungle" films in the late 1930s, she became famous for wearing a Hollywood-ized version of a pareu, dubbed a sarong. And despite playing many other roles (and the many other actresses who wore the costume, too), Lamour was never able to shake the "sarong girl" nickname she acquired after her biggest hit, "The Hurricane" (1937).

Neither the pareu nor the sarong would have much impact on Hawaiian-made garments themselves, but the unique and distinctive pareu patterns would prove extremely popular and long-lived for fabric designs. The plain, almost stark designs were classic enough to never quite go out of fashion, and from the time of the aloha shirt's invention in the 1930s until today, Tahitian prints have been standards.

Another Hawai'i tradition, the palaka print, has old roots, and, like the pareu, it was invented and manufactured elsewhere. Shirts came to Hawai'i in the 18th century, and spread as Westerners increasingly interacted with Hawaiians economically, first in the sandalwood trade, then whaling. Sailors landing in the islands wore loose-fitting, long-sleeved upper garments called frocks. It is commonly thought that the Hawaiians transliterated the word "frock" into "palaka." The pattern that became known as palaka is a heavy cotton cloth woven in a white and dark-blue plaid; over time, the term

Dorothy Lamour became famous for the numerous tropical movies she made, starting in the late 1930s. Inevitably in these films - as here, in 1941 - she was dressed in a sarong.

Pineapples and a scanty pareu are supposed to lend this young woman a Hawaiian appearance. Adorning a 1954 calendar, she was painted by commercial artist Earl Moran for the Brown & Bigelow Co.

This little girl
Is one big reason
Hawaii is grand
In any season.

came to be used to define not the shirt, but the fabric. (It has also been conjectured that the word palaka could be based on the word "block," referring to the appearance of the rectangular design.) By the end of the 19th century, as immigrants came to Hawai'i to work in the fields and mills, the use of palaka spread because of its durability, coolness, and design.

Tailored shirts with collars and buttons up the front had already been brought into Hawai'i by American businessmen, and they served as design inspiration for palaka shirts and jackets, which were more closely fitting garments than the frock shirt. Palaka shirts were commonly worn by plantation workers, who needed the thick cloth to protect against the sharp edges of sugarcane leaves or spiny pineapple tops. But laborers of all types wore palaka by 1900. Within a few decades many residents felt an affection for the local associations that palaka had, and it was adopted for wear by teenagers and young adults who did no heavy physical work. Eventually, by the 1970s, some descendants of the original immigrant field workers came to see palaka as a symbol of their families' early struggles. By then, the now-closed Arakawa's Department Store ("in the proud plantation town of Waipahu," as their widespread advertising boasted) specialized in palaka garments made not only in the traditional white and navy blue, but also in red, green, black, and even purple and pink. (The store, which opened in 1909, was continuing a tradition since it had originally supplied "real" palaka work shirts to plantation workers.)

Another element in Hawai'i's evolving garment industry appeared in the 1920s although at first this would not be so significant for the soon-to-appear

Above: The pattern's the same as always, but the glowing pink color and tapered cut of this shirt show that it was made in the 1960s. Right: A 1980s palaka shirt made by Arakawa's (Right only: University of Hawai'i's CTAHR Historic Costume Collection).

aloha shirt. In 1922, two factories opened: the Union Supply Company and the Hawai'i Clothing Manufacturing Company. Both made work clothes used by civilians and the increasing number of military personnel in the islands. The latter company became known for its "sailor moku" pants, which were wide-legged with front buttons, resembling sailor pants except for their fabric, which was thick, dark-colored cotton or denim. Sailor mokus became popular for young people in the '20s and '30s, and in the latter decade were frequently worn with aloha shirts. As the alohawear industry began, the factory system established in the early 1920s would be used for shirts as well.

The influence of Hawai'i's many Asian immigrants was pivotal in the creation of the aloha shirt. In the early 20th century, immigrants were adapting to the customs of their new home in Hawai'i. Men and children often switched fairly quickly to wearing Western-style clothing for work or school, while adult women were more likely to retain their native garments. Travelers to Hawai'i often commented that this mixture added an exotic touch to the streets of Honolulu.

In many households, clothing was still sewn by wives and mothers, which created a demand for fabrics of different kinds to be stocked in stores. Among these were Chinese silks, which had long been exported to the West, and cottons, particularly calico and small-figured prints, were favorites from the mainland U.S. Also found in Hawai'i at this time was the Filipino men's shirt called the barong tagalong, made of pina, a cool, sheer fabric of pineapple fabric. Island laborers, who had little time for leisure and few Filipino women to socialize with (since comparatively few were allowed to come),

Above: A Union Supply Co. palaka work shirt from the 1960s. Below: An onlooker wearing a palaka shirt (circled) watches the famous Chinatown fire destroy part of downtown Honolulu in January 1900 (Bishop Museum).

Three kihikihi fish appear on a silk women's beach jacket. While such garments first were worn in the twenties, Hawaiian designs like this wouldn't appear till the 1930s.

would have had little chance to wear a dress-up garment like this. But this shirt, worn loose over trousers, could have been one of the inspirations for the aloha shirt's similar untucked style. (A 1950 newspaper article specifically credited Duke Kahanamoku with the innovation of a straight, "no-tails" shirt hem.)

Increasingly, Caucasian residents (and tourists) purchased non-Western ethnic clothing. In some cases this was bought purely for its novelty value as a costume, but by the late 1920s more and more haole (Caucasian) women chose Chinese outfits with pants (still not commonly worn by women then) for party wear, or covered their swimming attire with a Japanese silk coat called a haori. Although a fairly small influence, this showed how the migration of clothing styles didn't move just one way, from established Westerners to arriving Asians.

The Japanese came to be the largest ethnic group in Hawai'i by the time federal law stopped Asian immigration in 1924, and many Japanese opened their own small businesses as they moved away from plantation work. Tailoring was one of these lines of work, and the best-known tailor shop in Honolulu in the 1920s and '30s was Musa-shiya the Shirtmaker. The establishment became famous with a series of advertisements dreamed up by a Caucasian ad man, George Mellen, who created a caricature of a smiling, humble Japanese man who "spoke" (in print) in comically fractured English. (Interestingly, ads in publications aimed at local

In Japan, the haori (a type of silk coat) was meant to be worn over a kimono. Fashionable women in Hawai'i adapted it for other purposes, as shown by this 1929 advertisement.

Japanese did not use these gimmicks.) The advertisements successfully spread the store's name even to tourists. Both Western-style dress shirts and Japanese fabric were sold at Musa-Shiya—and the latter, wherever it was purchased, became the crucial element in the creation of the aloha shirt.

Traditional Japanese fabric patterns differed according to whom they were intended to be worn by, and in what time of year. Social rules governing these patterns were strictly defined: under most circumstances, men and older women wore only darker, mostly solid colors, but children and young women were permitted to use fabrics of bright colors and bold designs. In some cases, as on a woman's wedding kimono, patterns were very realistic, usually including flowers and leaves. Very young boys might be dressed in designs incorporating stronger, more masculine subjects, such as leaping carp or pieces of armor. Even the more abstract patterns that evolved around the turn of the century in Japan usually had similar gender or seasonal characteristics which defined whom they could be worn by. While silk was most commonly used, printed cottons were also popular during the warm months of the year. These yukata fabrics (plain white cotton with patterns usually in dark blue, often created by a tie-dyeing process) were also found in Hawai'i, where both men and women wore them in leisure times.

The well-known Musashiya fabric store advertised itself differently to varying audiences. For local Japanese, the grinning cartoon store proprietor (see p. 20) was omitted, as this 1941 ad shows.

Musashiya.   King St.

The humble Musashiya store in downtown Honolulu was significant in the development of the aloha shirt. In spite of its small size, it became famous due to advertisements like the one at right. The text in this 1934 example refers jokingly to seasickness, as it was published in a magazine used aboard Matson Lines' ships en route to Hawai'i from the west coast (Top: Bishop Museum).

Musa-shiya the Shirtmaker speaking

Maybe today your protested me offer shirt conversation, caused of unpleasured feelings which most people usually obtain at a stomach on ocean water. Tomorrow maybe burst open inform for my shirt, kimono, pajamma, etc and etc Honolulu. Hoping your favorably attention on tomorrow advertisement with this few word I thank you.

1954 beauty contest winner Miss Aloha Maui (left) examines Japanese-print fabric while Christmas shopping in a Maui store.

Three early aloha shirts from the middle to late 1930s are made of light cotton cloth printed in Japanese motifs.

Japanese fabric used to make kimonos, which were still being worn at least occasionally by some women in Hawai'i even into the 1930s, was traditionally only 14-inches wide—too narrow for Western-style garments like shirts. But fabric in Western widths (twice that size), using many traditional, established Japanese motifs, was also made in Japan, and this was exported to Hawai'i as well.

Different types of fabric could be purchased in the islands at this time. Silks of various weights and qualities were available, with different degrees of colorfastness. Not all silk was the smooth, slippery kind; one variety known as kabe crepe had a rougher, pebbled surface. (In years to come this would be popular for aloha shirts.) Less expensive, and used far more for most clothing, was cotton. Rayon, the first synthetic

Japanese designs have always been popular for aloha shirts. Fabric with floral motifs (at left) would only have been used for girls' kimonos in Japan; for aloha shirts, such rules didn't apply (University of Hawai'i's CTAHR Historic Costume Collection).

This fabric is kabe crepe, a particular type of silk with a slightly textured surface. The mixed images are all typically Japanese.

Oiled-paper umbrellas and calligraphy are featured on this cotton fabric from the late 1950s.

fiber, then resembled today's nylon tricot and was generally used most often for inexpensive undergarments. It was manufactured in both Japan and the U.S., but was not yet of sufficient quality to be suitable for printing and could not retain vivid colors. (It was not until the 1940s that heavier rayon would be made; the collectible rayon aloha shirts that are most sought today date from the postwar years.)

Japanese silks and cottons were used to make the earliest aloha shirts—and that revolutionary step was about to be taken.

The darker colors and forceful designs seen here would traditionally have been considered entirely masculine in Japanese culture (University of Hawai'i's CTAHR Historic Costume Collection).

How Fabric is Printed

ndividual Hand-blocked prints in designs of your own choice
EXCLUSIVE WITH YOU !

Tina Leser's
Designing Salon
2322 Kalakaua Ave.

B

In alohawear's early days, some designs were hand-blocked, like this dress that was advertised in 1939.

Without printed fabric, aloha shirts cannot exist. How designs get onto fabric in turn determines what kind of garments can be made.

Hawai'i has never had a large enough population to support much really large-scale manufacturing. Furthermore, it has consistently found itself unable to compete with other places in the world in terms of keeping costs low, so numerous successful businesses have eventually been undercut by outside (cheaper) competition. This has been true for the garment industry in particular.

With few options to manufacture printed fabric locally, the first approach was the most low-tech method possible: hand-painting. Today such work would be prohibitively expensive, but in the 1930s and '40s, individually hand-painted garments were available. Stencils were likely used for at least part of the design to reduce labor. The output has to have been small, and surviving garments are rare, but sweatshirts and men's bathing suits are known to have been produced. (Men's neckties decorated with hula dancers are not as rare, but, despite their subject matter, these were manufactured on the mainland.)

The next option, which offered at least some degree of mass production, was hand-blocking. In this, a design is cut by hand onto a surface, then the surface is inked and pressed onto fabric. Such a design must, of necessity, be fairly simple, meaning that it can look crude (if poorly done) or graphically bold, if successful. Hand-blocking is a slow process and unsuitable for producing a large amount of material, but in its time it filled a niche market in Hawai'i for fabrics of

different types. The very first hand-blocked cloth seems to have been made starting in the middle '30s by upscale retailers Gump's and the East India Store for curtains and upholstery, tablecloths and napkins, and some garments. During World War II, when military personnel were eager to buy souvenirs but manufacturing and shipping were badly disrupted, less skillful hand-blocked pieces were produced in quantity. These seem to mostly have been scarves or tablecloths, or even just pieces of unfinished, inexpensive fabric probably sold as table runners. Popular wartime motifs were hula dancers and tropical fish.

Hal Davis and Harvey Dukelow silk-screen a design incorporating Marquesan tikis at Hawaiian Hand Prints in Honolulu in 1949. The fabric could be used for upholstery, or for shirts like the ones they're wearing. (Ray Jerome Baker, Bishop Museum)

This tablecloth (above) and satin scarf (below) are locally-made World War II souvenirs with silk-screened Hawaiian designs.

Moving upward in sophistication is silk-screening. Like hand-blocking, this too is low-tech and requires much hand labor, but the printed results can look far crisper and more professional. Silk-screening also offers the potential to add more colors (screened and applied separately). On the downside, though, both methods require careful handling since spilled or smeared ink can ruin the print, and they could only be used on thicker fabrics such as cotton, not on rayon or silk. Yet some substantial silk-screening operations existed in Hawai'i in the 1940s and '50s. Their output ranged from motifs printed individually on finished garments (a small logo on a front pocket, or the entire back of a bowling shirt) to lengthy strips of uncut cloth. Despite a period of successful silk-screening in Hawai'i, the typical pattern unfolded and eventually local production couldn't compete with outside manufacturers.

Last of the processes is roller-printing. In this, metal rollers are etched with designs, dye is applied, then fabric runs over the rollers to pick up dyes. This is how most cloth receives patterns, including that used for the earliest aloha shirts. But this process is only done in

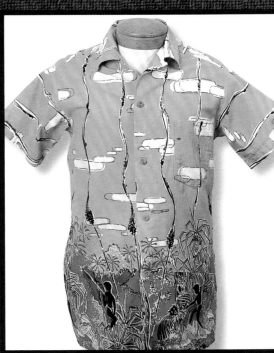

Early silk-screening in Hawai'i sometimes looked fairly crude, but Alfred Shaheen's work in the 1950s and '60s was both skillfully executed and strikingly designed. (University of Hawai'i's CTAHR Historic Costume Collection)

Two examples of typical Hawai'i silk-screening: the design on the blue fabric runs along the bottom of a jack shirt; the red cloth has accents in metallic silver ink.

large factories that never existed in Hawai'i, so local garment manufacturers had to order this type of cloth from the mainland or Japan. The latter had the advantage of requiring far smaller runs (3,000 yards vs. 10,000 yards from the U.S., for instance), but ordering from either location required months for printing and shipping; once received, the bulky rolls needed to be stored before they were slowly used up as shirts were sewn. Even with this disadvantage, roller-printing still produced the nice-looking results most customers wanted, and was therefore still considered the best method.

THE ALOHA SHIRT
The Debut: the 1930s

The invention of the aloha shirt was of some significance in the history of Hawai'i, if only because it eventually spawned an entire industry that would employ thousands. But, interestingly, the inception itself will always be a mystery. That's because no one person or company can be identified as the aloha shirt's inventor, nor can any definite date even be determined for its first appearance.

This historical uncertainty is in contrast to mainstream fashion in the 20th century, where changes in clothing styles are usually fairly easy to date. As a rule, new clothes were introduced at well-attended and publicized fashion shows at designer salons; then women's magazines, Hollywood films, and advertisements spread awareness of new styles, creating a process that left a clear historical record.

But the aloha shirt didn't follow these rules. There was no designer to introduce it, and when it did come into being, the local press at first paid little attention. That was because the aloha shirt began "on the street" and not in someone's design studio, and perhaps not even from one single source. The basic ingredients for its creation were in place in Honolulu: the colorful fabric was for sale in stores, and skilled seamstresses and tailors were already at work. It just remained for the two to interact.

Various dates have been proposed for the debut of the first aloha shirts. Some people have suggested the late 1920s—occasional reminiscences from people who lived then have described such garments as being worn. But exhaustive research of dated photos from that time has

Some significant business names in the aloha shirt story appear in this group of 1930s labels used on Hawai'i-manufactured garments.

never shown anything like an aloha shirt. Although collectors and writers from more recent years have frequently repeated this date for surviving shirts, it must be doubted; any few such examples that might have been made in the ʻ20s are unlikely to still exist.

Aloha shirts as we know them were, in fact, invented in the 1930s. Who first did this, and when, will never be known for certain this many years later. It could have been a Japanese mother, using scraps of kimono fabric to make a shirt for her little boy. Or a beachboy from Waikīkī, looking for something splashy to wear to a party. Or an adventurous tourist who picked some eye-catching cloth in a store that made shirts to order. Or a young Filipino plantation worker who loved bright colors. Or it might very well have been a high-school student from a well-to-do kamaʻaina (long-time resident) family who wanted to show off. Whoever did it, it was done in the early 1930s, and it first started a fad, and then a whole industry.

The bathing suit worn by the girl at center in this circa 1937 photo is made from one of the earliest known Hawaiian fabric prints. The pattern mimics luggage stickers and tourist advertising (N. R. Farbman, Bishop Museum).

A convivial group photographed around 1938, possibly at the Pearl Harbor Yacht Club, is dressed mostly in tropical or Hawaiian-patterned silk shirts. Such designs were still fairly new on the market at that time.

The first aloha shirts were likely made to order, but this doesn't mean they were tailored to fit a specific person based on individual measurements, as the term might imply today. Instead, they were merely shirts of standard sizes—small, medium, large—made in a fabric the customer selected from bolts of material displayed in the store. So these were not prestigious, expensive pieces of clothing; Musa-shiya briefly advertised shirts like this costing as little as 75 cents. Tourists could order a shirt on their arrival and have it made quickly enough to wear for their entire stay.

The next step in this story was the switch from shirts sewn one at a time for specific orders to those already made up and stocked for immediate sale. This progression is attributed to Ellery Chun, who recalled in later years that he began doing this at King-Smith, his family's store in downtown Honolulu, in 1932 or '33.

We know shirts with Japanese motifs existed first, and were popular for many years afterward. But perhaps a more important question is when the first

This Royal Hawaiian brand cotton shirt dates from 1937, and its pattern depicts pages from tourist publications. The pullover con-struction was popular in the earliest years of the aloha shirt (University of Hawai'i's CTAHR Historic Costume Collection).

Three types of aloha shirt fabric designs appear in this scene from the 1944 Hollywood film "Tahiti Nights": traditional Japanese (far left), pareu (2nd from right), and tropical/Hawaiian (far right) (What's happening with the man in the center is not as easily explained.).

Hawaiian fabric was made. Again, we don't know for sure. Locally handmade Hawaiian-patterned textiles were marketed in 1935, but these were intended for use as upholstery and curtains, not for clothing. Material for garments was definitely in existence by 1937, when photos were taken of clothes made of printed broadcloth cotton bearing a design mimicking Hawaiian luggage stickers and which could have been manufactured in the U.S. But also common in this very early period were Japanese silk or cotton shirts, occasionally in a pullover style, with some Hawaiian designs (hula dancers, grass houses) or generic tropical ones

Carved wooden containers were invented for Hawaiian perfumes first sold by Gump's in the 1930s. These, however, are lower-cost copies made later by other local manufacturers.

(palm trees, sailboats, fish.) Ellen Chun Lum, the sister of Ellery Chun and a significant figure in the aloha shirt saga, created Hawaiian fabric designs that were printed onto silk to be sold at the King-Smith store at this time. Pictures from 1938 show patterned shirts like these, and a 1939 magazine advertisement is illustrated with a photo of the classic type of shirt. By then, more than one published account describes Hawaiian-patterned shirts. More research may eventually pinpoint an unquestionable birth year. However, this may never happen since the evidence left to us—historic photos (not too rare) and surviving shirts (very rare)—can be extremely difficult to date with

The boy's silk shirt in the center was purchased in Honolulu in the middle 1930s. Seashells and malolo (flying fish) make up the pattern. The shirts behind it (also silk) date from the 1940s and '50s.

The 1930s saw the creation of a distinctive local or Hawaiian style, not only in clothing like aloha shirts but in etched glass items like this platter with an image of a night blooming cereus blossom.

certainty so many decades later.

Whatever the exact date of their first appearance, by the late '30s aloha shirts were seen frequently. In *Hawaiian Holiday*, a children's fiction book published on the mainland in 1938, a wealthy New York family visits Hawai'i. On a shopping trip to downtown Honolulu, mother and daughter encounter something new: "In another shop they found the shirts which so many of the men and girls in Honolulu wear. They are called *Aloha* shirts and they are made in bright colors with lively figures. When the children first saw them they could not believe that men would wear anything so gay [gay still meant bright, lively], but they soon became used to them." Two shirts are purchased, one with "a green and white background with black boats on it" and the other "with a bright purple background and little boys riding hobbyhorses on it." Mother comments, "'I'll certainly be able to find my sons when I want to...You can see these a mile away.'" The recipients are "delighted with their *Aloha* shirts. 'I can't wait to wear mine,' Jimmy said."

The arrival of Hawaiian print fabric coincided with a general boom of artistic Hawaiian awareness in the 1930s; this, in fact, marks the beginning of the pride in being "local" that would continue to grow in later years. Instead of simply copying or importing mainland styles, local designers began to look to their own surroundings, including different facets of the varying ethnic cultures in the islands, for inspiration. Not only fabrics, but also jewelry, furniture, and commercial art evolved to focus on subjects found in Hawai'i.

The birth of this movement occurred at the Gump's store, located at Lewers Road and Kalākaua Avenue in Waikīkī. Gump's opened in 1929 and originally sold mostly Asian merchandise, catering to the upscale tourists attracted to the newly-opened Royal Hawaiian Hotel as well as to wealthy residents. But in the early 1930s Gump's pursued a different direction, commissioning artists to create Hawaiian-type designs for etched glass pieces, silverware, and carved wood furniture and smaller objects. Starting in 1935, they also sold hand-blocked fabrics for curtains and upholstery. In most cases, the favored local motifs were tropical flowers. The popularity of this new Gump's merchandise insured that lower-cost imitations quickly appeared (and indeed, long outlasted the originals.) With this boom in uniquely Hawaiian products, aloha shirts fit in nicely.

It should be pointed out that aloha shirts represented a notable development in men's fashions. Depending on their job or social status, men in America (and Hawaiʻi) for many years wore solid-color shirts, usually white, sometimes accented with a colorful necktie or bandana. Stripes or plaids might occasionally be seen, but it was virtually unknown for a man to wear a shirt bearing, for example, flower designs or any other recognizable image. Even in the freewheeling 1920s, a brightly colored patterned bathrobe was considered quite unusual. Aloha shirts changed all that, first as to what men could wear as leisure attire, and eventually—in Hawaiʻi, at least—as to what men could wear to work. (Another gender-related change aloha shirts brought: the wearing of one virtually identical garment by both men and women.)

McInerny, a leading island clothing store, boasted that it sold "the ultimate in Hawai'i's own sport togs" like the alohawear worn by the couple on the left in this 1939 ad.

By this time, the company had already expanded from its original downtown Honolulu location to a resort shop at the Royal Hawaiian Hotel to sell specifically to tourists.

The question arises as to where the term "aloha shirt" came from. (Mainland people, with justification, have pretty much always just called the garments Hawaiian shirts.) In the mid-1930s the word "aloha" was attached to many types of merchandise, often intended partly for tourists—there were "aloha" tea sets and "aloha" coasters—so the term was not originally used for sportswear. The phrase was first published by Musa-Shiya the Shirtmaker, who advertised in the *Honolulu Advertiser* on June 28, 1935, "Aloha shirts—well tailored, beautiful designs and radiant colors." However, it was Ellery Chun who trademarked the term "aloha shirt" in 1937; because the King-Smith store was doing well selling the shirts, he noted in an article in a 1978 GQ magazine, "I figured it was a good idea to own the trademark."

The year 1936 was pivotal: two major garment manufacturers, Kamehameha and Branfleet, opened factories to produce sportswear. Even though some people wore the new styles, sales to the local population

Charlie Chan was a famous fictional Honolulu detective; this store's proprietor was a real person who happened to have the same name. In this 1939 ad are men's trunks with a handpainted hula girl design and an aloha shirt with an early "chop suey" print.

Aloha shirts went national in this 1942 fashion illustration from Esquire magazine which shows a smart young couple dressed in identical "Hawaiian printed silk shirts". This was still just a preliminary, for the mainland wouldn't really pay attention to the style till the early 1950s.

were comparatively sluggish; the major buyers of aloha shirts were tourists in Hawai'i (and eventually, in the prewar years, consumers on the U.S. mainland). Due to economic conditions, Hawai'i residents were focused on their need for work clothing: Hawai'i was still a plantation economy, with the bulk of its population primarily in the lower classes; only the upper classes could afford (or had need for) clothing for leisure activities.

Kamehameha was the dominant garment manufacturer in the 1930s, and an anthurium print shirt it created then was on raw silk. Recalled Herb Briner in a 1961 newspaper article, "It was the beginning and almost the end of Kamehameha … because of the unstable quality of the imported fabric." Dyes faded on raw silk, so Briner came up with an alternative: a type of cotton grown in Peru that had practically no shrinkage. The cotton was shipped to Japan for printing and then back to Kamehameha in Hawai'i, where it was sewn into garments. The switch to more dependable yardage allowed the successful launching of prints for Island sportswear.

Originally a small plant in Honolulu that manufactured men's raw silk shirts, Kamehameha grew and the company relocated from the island of O'ahu to Hilo, on the Big Island of Hawai'i, where there was a ready pool of trained seamstresses. Briner served as president and handled local sales, while Millie Briner designed for the firm. In the early years, their fabrics were designed in Hawai'i, printed in California, and then manufactured into shirts back in Hawai'i. During the Christmas season of 1936, a shipping strike stranded the fabric in California, with some of the finished garments in Hawai'i. The companies tried to sell the goods

daily double

No, you're not seeing double. But on second thought, perhaps you are. Even the number two on the doubling cube is significant as this twosome plays backgammon in a patio at a winter resort. It carries out the idea of pairs, setting the fashion theme. It's no longer a secret that the women have appropriated many styles of wearables from men's wardrobes, including shorts for tennis, raglan raincoats, reversible coats, slacks, covert cloth coats and suits, Shetland jackets, sweaters . . . but you get the idea, so why go on. The outgrowth of this neat bit of filching seems to be the increasingly popular custom of matching outfits for him and her. The dice-shaker (that's the male member of the duo, if you're having trouble) wears the Hawaiian printed silk shirt, a pair of Harbor Blue washable slacks and Sandune ribbed anklets. The tooled design on the tongue of his moccasin slippers brings a new note to footwear. The girl's ensemble duplicates his, with the exception of the moccasins, which are untooled. Even the two Scotties are a bit bewildered by this new fashion trend.

(For answers to your dress queries, send stamped self-addressed envelope to Esquire Fashion Staff, 366 Madison Ave., N. Y.)

Aloha ... Hawaii !

That word on the label is pronounced Ka-may-ha-may-ha (it's the name of Hawaii's
greatest King) ... and the playclothes are as authentic as the name. Kamehameha
fashions are styled and made right in Hawaii (where else is there so much inspiration for romance
under the sun?) ... of famed fabrics that thrive on sun and water. At one fine store in each city.

KAMEHAMEHA GARMENT COMPANY, Ltd. · Honolulu 2, Hawaii

Kamehameha was
an important
manufacturer of
alohawear; this
stylish 1947 ad was
published both
locally and on the
mainland, where
readers were
helpfully instructed
on how to pro-
nounce the firm's
name.

locally but residents did not buy enough—the "local" identity, which in years to come would provide support for the aloha shirt, was as yet fairly undeveloped. So the fledgling apparel industry began exporting aloha attire; only five percent of their garments were sold locally. A 1939 article in the *Honolulu Advertiser* boasted that the local garment industry had grown to "million dollar proportions" since 1937, and that Kamehameha produced "23 exclusive print designs ... all of the cottons being printed on the U.S. mainland."

Branfleet (later renamed Kahala Sportswear) was founded, also in 1936, by George Brangier and Nat Norfleet. Today, like Kamehameha, Kahala is one of the oldest and largest such firms in the islands. Along with Kamehameha, the company began by selling aloha shirts made of kabe crepes in Asian designs. They were also the first to supply sportswear to the U.S. mainland on a large scale. By 1939, the most popular prints were still quite subtle, with small motifs and little color contrast. With slight modifications, these basic designs were used through the end of World War II. Branfleet's company trademark was the "pineapple tweed." The fabric looked like rough linen; it was durable, and was constructed into

plain, solid-colored shirts with long sleeves and open collars, which were also referred to as jackets. The only decoration was the Hawaiian crest with the motto, "The life of the land is perpetuated in righteousness." This also marked the first appearance of clothing to use the name of Duke Kahanamoku; although short-lived, much more of this would come in later years.

Aiming specifically to fulfill tourist demand was the Royal Hawaiian Manufacturing Company, founded in 1937 by Max Lewis. Motifs on the early Royal Hawaiian aloha shirts tended to be very bold Hawaiian designs. Some of the earliest labeled proto-Hawaiian shirts come from Royal Hawaiian Manufacturing.

George Brangier was one of the founders of Branfleet, which later became Kahala Sportswear. Here he and a helper handle Japanese-fabric aloha shirts in the 1930s (Hawai'i State Archives).

ABOVE: THE KAHALA DISTRICT OF THE CITY OF HONOLULU BEGAN AS A PLEASANT, UPPER MIDDLE CLASS BEACH SUBURB IN THE 1920s BUT GREW TO BE MUCH MORE UPSCALE. BELOW: THERE HAVE BEEN TWO HISTORIC HOTELS WITH THE ROYAL HAWAIIAN NAME; THE FIRST WAS LOCATED IN DOWNTOWN HONOLULU FROM THE 1870s TO THE EARLY PART OF THE 20TH CENTURY. THE MORE FAMILIAR ONE IS TODAY'S ROYAL HAWAIIAN HOTEL IN WAIKIKI, WHICH OPENED IN 1927.

Duke Kahanamoku

Duke Kahanamoku, arguably the best-known Hawaiian person in history, made his mark most notably in sports. A significant contributor to the revival of surfing at Waikiki in the early 1900s, he caused an even bigger splash by competing in four Olympic Games, winning multiple medals and dazzling the swimming world with his first triumphs at the 1912 Olympics in Stockholm, Sweden. Hobnobbing with movie stars and the famous politicians who invariably sought his company when they visited the islands, Duke symbolized Hawaiian culture to millions throughout America and the world. And remarkably, decades after his death in 1968, his fame remains strong.

Interestingly, Duke had a major role in the world of the aloha shirt as well. He licensed his name three times for use on various types of garments, and was publicized as having a hand in designing clothes and selecting fabric patterns, too. Duke Kahanamoku-labeled merchandise was sold as follows:

1937-1942: Branfleet (later Kahala) made plain, unprinted cotton shirts and jackets in their signature rough-textured "pineapple tweed" and solid-color trunks, decorated only with embroidered patches using a design based on the Hawaiian crest first used by Hawai'i's royalty in the 1800s. At

Duke Kahanamoku licensed his name for a variety of commercial ventures. Above is a brochure for a popular 1960s Waikiki nightclub; at right is a 1964 clothing ad.

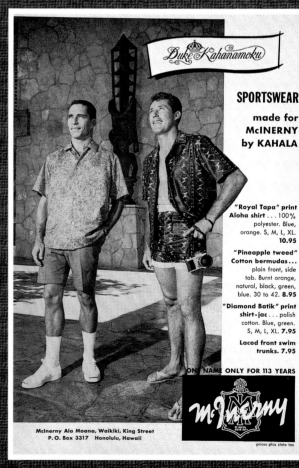

SPORTSWEAR made for McINERNY by KAHALA

"Royal Tapa" print Aloha shirt . . . 100% polyester. Blue, orange. S, M, L, XL. **10.95**

"Pineapple tweed" Cotton bermudas . . . plain front, side tab. Burnt orange, natural, black, green, blue. 30 to 42. **8.95**

"Diamond Batik" print shirt-jac . . . polish cotton. Blue, green. S, M, L, XL. **7.95**

Laced front swim trunks. 7.95

ONE NAME ONLY FOR 113 YEARS

McInerny Ala Moana, Waikiki, King Street
P. O. Box 3317   Honolulu, Hawaii

prices plus state tax

The earliest Duke Kahanamoku shirts bore pocket patches like this one, which happens to have come from Duke's home.

least some of the patches carried Duke's name across the bottom. Swim trunks of this kind had already been made by a specialty tailor, Linn's, in Waikiki. The style (with distinctive white or colored stripes down the side) remained popular into the 1960s. Embroidered patches with the crest design were on the market into the 1950s as well, long after this initial batch of Duke clothing, although they usually said ROYAL HAWAIIAN (used by the company of the same name) or a generic ALOHA HAWAI'I. Duke was later credited for inventing the straight-hemmed shirt (which these were) with no tails to tuck in that was meant to be worn loose.

1949-1961: Cisco, a mainland manufacturer, used Duke's name on the labels of rayon shirts made in scores of different patterns. These are the most famous of the Duke-logoed clothing, and, as examples of the more "classic" aloha shirts, they have been considered collectible for some time. The most famous is the one worn by Montgomery Clift in his death scene in the 1954 film "From Here to Eternity." To publicize this venture Duke made promotional trips to the mainland beginning in early 1950 to

VINTAGE DUKE KAHANAMOKU SHIRTS COME WITH DIFFERENT LABELS. THOSE MADE BY CISCO IN THE 1950s ARE IDENTIFIED BY THE EXAMPLE SHOWN ABOVE CENTER. LATER GARMENT LABELS FROM THE '60S (TOP AND BOTTOM, ABOVE) HAVE THE SAME SCRIPT LOGO THAT CAN BE FOUND ON OTHER DUKE MERCHANDISE FROM THE SAME PERIOD.

On a promotional tour for his line of alohawear, Duke Kahanamoku visits a Los Angeles store in 1950 (Victor Barnaba, Bishop Museum).

introduce the new shirts, and later he wore them for multiple photos, posing with visiting celebrities including Clark Gable and Arthur Godfrey.

1961-1968: As part of a larger licensing scheme that put his name on a variety of products, Duke returned to Kahala, the same company that did his first garments (under their original name of Branfleet.) The most popular of the 1960s Duke shirts seem to have been cotton pareu prints. The label used the same script logotype that also appeared as the name of the well-known nightclub in the International Market Place in Waikiki, as well as on merchandise including surfboards, skateboards, and even aloha print canvas sneakers.

Tropical props accent a window display of Duke shirts at Silverwoods in Los Angeles in 1950. Small signs price the shirts at $6.95 each (Dick Whittington, Bishop Museum).

THE DEVELOPMENT OF AN INDUSTRY: THE 1940S AND '50S

The early years of the alohawear industry saw heartening levels of growth, as the U.S. and Hawai'i economies continued to improve after the terrible troubles of the Great Depression. In 1941, both strong tourism and increasing military spending contributed to economic good times. But the sudden and shocking tragedy of the war's arrival in Hawai'i on December 7, 1941, overturned all usual business practices.

The years of World War II brought major disruptions and then, after a time, a business boom. Obviously, with Japan at war with the United States, all commerce between the two countries ceased and no fabric could be imported from Japan. Meanwhile, at home in America, demands for the immense undertaking of fighting a global war meant that every industry made changes in what it produced, raw materials were hard or impossible to get, and all forms of shipping were slowed. The needs of civilian retailers were, of necessity, sometimes ignored. In Hawai'i in the first months of the war, the immediate problem, especially for those dependent on tourism, was that there were no visitors. The U.S. Navy controlled all travel to and from the islands, and pleasure trips were absolutely prohibited. But as the war proceeded and the fighting moved farther away

Proud to be the first local Japanese inductee accepted into the U.S. Army, Mitsuru Doi poses with his parents and baby sister on Kauai in 1943 (Prejudice had kept Hawai'i's Japanese men out of the service for the first few years of World War II.). His aloha shirt depicts the main Hawaiian Islands (Library of Congress).

WIFE

The dearest and best in the world to me—
You take your place in the world each day
In a very sacred and honored way
With thousands of love ones far and near
Each held precious and very dear
And, to you, these loving words of mine
Pay a tribute on every line
To the Wonderful Wife who'll always be

ALOHA HAWAII

All the expected Hawaiian subjects (a hula girl, grass house, Diamond Head) accompany a poem to a "Wonderful Wife" silk-screened on this satin World War II-era scarf.

in the Pacific, more and more military personnel arrived. They proved to be great customers, with paychecks in their pockets and a sometimes fatalist attitude of wanting to spend some

dough before they shipped out to battle. Lots of them wanted souvenirs to send to the folks back home, and these new buyers eventually more than made up for the loss of tourists.

But what to sell them? Merchandise was hard to get. Many of the souvenirs had to be made locally, and this included some amount of clothing. Undoubtedly most of this was likely cotton, and while some tropical prints were probably manufactured on the mainland and sold in Hawai'i during those years, other material presumably was somehow printed locally. Known wartime souvenirs are mostly hand-blocked or silk-screened napkins, tablecloths, and some scarves. With war-time restrictions, including federal rationing that dictated the amounts of cloth that could be used for

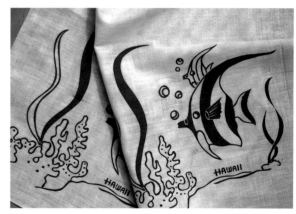

Locally-produced wartime souvenir tablecloths bear simple silk-screened Hawaiian designs.

certain types of garments, patterned shirts were probably not plentiful. Even after the war ended, normal business conditions for Hawai'i's garment industry returned only gradually, partly because Japan would need several years to rebuild its ruined economy. Restoring tourism was slowed by the rundown condition of both hotel accommodations and the Matson Lines ships most visitors traveled on, which the Navy used throughout the war and were very much the worse for wear. Military personnel who saw Hawai'i during the war had arrived with many preconceived notions of what they'd encounter in "paradise." Just about all of them had heard Hawaiian music on the radio, watched Hollywood films set in the South Seas, or at least seen some carnival sideshow "hula" dancer back home. Many were disappointed with the sometimes dreary reality of wartime Hawai'i, and complained of crowded business establishments that just seemed to want to grab their money for inferior merchandise. Many swore they never wanted to see "the rock" (a derogatory name for O'ahu) again. But with the passage of a few years, many of these veterans mellowed, and eventually began to

return, this time as tourists. They'd be one of the factors in the national craze for Hawaiian things (including clothing) that would arrive in the 1950s.

Starting before the war, major U.S. fabric manufacturers began making drapery and upholstery fabric with bold designs of tropical foliage. This remained fashionable well into the 1940s, coinciding with the popularity of rattan furniture manufactured in the Philippines. Rattan became universally used throughout Hawai'i and its popularity spread to warm areas of the mainland, and this fabric worked perfectly for covering the cushions used on rattan pieces. In the islands, an additional niche market developed for shirts made of this heavy printed fabric, produced by Wong's Draperies. These shirts were worn by local residents, never by tourists, and although they were not advertised, they remained popular from the 1940s through the 1960s. The thick fabric could sometimes be too warm for Hawai'i, but it was popular with local students who attended mainland colleges.

A gradual change in alohawear began in the late 1940s at the first stirrings of the breakdown in the heretofore rigid requirements of

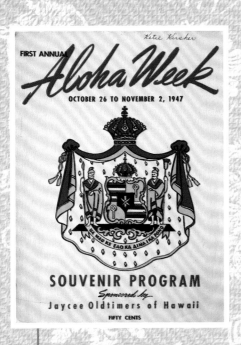

First Annual
Aloha Week
OCTOBER 26 TO NOVEMBER 2, 1947

SOUVENIR PROGRAM
Sponsored by
Jaycee Oldtimers of Hawaii
FIFTY CENTS

COLORFUL YEARLY EVENTS THAT CONSISTENTLY DRAW TOURISTS ARE THE DELIGHT OF THOSE WHO DEPEND ON VISITOR DOLLARS. THE FLORAL PARADE AND MID-PACIFIC CARNIVAL WERE VERY POPULAR IN THE EARLY 1900s, TILL WORLD WAR I ENDED THEM. ATTEMPTS TO REVIVE THE IDEA WERE UNSUCCESSFUL IN THE LATE 1920s (THE ALOHA FESTIVAL) AND 1939 (THE HOʻOLAULEA). ALOHA WEEK (TODAY KNOWN AS THE ALOHA FESTIVALS) HAS BEEN THE LONGEST-LIVED EVENT BY FAR, BEGINNING IN 1947 AND CONTINUING TO THE PRESENT.

An exuberant cartoon man jumps out of his uncomfortable suit into an aloha shirt in 1954 ("Right on the Kini Popo" was a local expression that meant "right on the ball.").

Right on the Kini-Popo . . . "Island" Prints . . . Fabrics . . . and Fashions

men's business attire. In Hawaiʻi, as throughout the United States, a man with a desk job wore nothing other than a tie and jacket—better yet, a suit—in a dark color. Even a sport jacket with some kind of subtle pattern was considered unacceptable. In this environment, the push to allow aloha shirts at work was initially quite a battle—but the skirmishes in an effort that would take decades to achieve success were beginning.

In 1946 the Honolulu Chamber of Commerce appropriated $1,000 to study aloha shirts and prepare suitable designs for clothing businessmen could wear during the hot summer months. A resolution was passed that allowed City & County of Honolulu employees to wear sport shirts from June through October each year, but the aloha shirt was specifically excluded. The resolution permitted "open-collar sport shirts in plain shades, but not the ones with the loud colorful designs and patterns."

In the following year came the next step, when the first Aloha Week celebration took place. Aloha Week arose from a mixture of cultural and economic motives. Honolulu businessman Harry Nordmark felt Hawaiian cultural practices needed to be re-instituted. "I thought it was a pity that none of this pageantry was left," he said. "The glory of ancient Hawaiʻi was behind museum walls. The public was forgetting that such music, dancing and philosophy of life ever

existed." But in addition to the aspirations of a cultural revival, Aloha Week was a sound economic plan: it was scheduled for October, a slow month for tourism, and it was designed to attract visitors.

Another major aspect of Aloha Week was the widespread expectation that employees of nearly all businesses and even government offices would wear casual aloha attire—the more colorful the better—for the entire week. While this was undeniably fun, the actual intent was to

Employees of the T. H. Davies office in Hilo show off alohawear instead of their usual business attire during Aloha Week 1949 (Bishop Museum).

SHIRTMAKERS OFFER
THEIR WARES IN THE
MIDDLE 1950s. ABOVE,
SATO CLOTHIERS
INFORMS MAIL ORDER
CUSTOMERS THAT
"PATTERN CHOICE
INCLUDES SCENERIES,
FLORALS, ANIMALS."
(THESE ARE JAPANESE
SILKS, NOT HAWAIIAN
PRINTS.) BELOW,
ISLAND APPAREL'S
SPECIALTY "ONE OF A
KIND" SHIRTS
PROBABLY WERE MADE
TO ORDER.

The "chop suey" print
was invented in the
1930s, mostly fell out of
favor by the late 1950s,
and returned in the late
1970s. It's still around.

benefit Hawai'i's fashion industry, which was producing all those mu'umu'u and aloha shirts. A prospectus for the first Aloha Week in 1947, prepared by the sponsoring organization (the Jaycee Oldtimers of Hawai'i) looked forward to "...participation by all organizations and citizens of the Territory in the wearing of Aloha shirts, Hawaiian prints, mu'umu'us, holokūs, etc...." These hopes were successfully realized, and this short respite from the usual office garb was so pleasant that many people commemorated it in the festival's early years by posing for group photos dressed in their special Aloha Week outfits. The first major break from drab business attire had come, and the trend would continue. (As would Aloha Week itself.)

The postwar period also saw the dawn of what would become known as classic (and later, collectible) aloha shirts, appreciated by connoisseurs for several decades. An improved rayon became common in the late 1940s, and was favored for these clothes. Rayon had been avoided in the prewar period because, as manufacturer Alfred Shaheen noted, "[it] was garbage...It was flimsy and inexpensive...they came out with a rayon that was heavier, and it finally held the dyes. Rayon shirts with a smooth finish and Hawaiian prints were only seen after World War II. No one was printing that stuff before the war."

This marked the real pinnacle of aloha shirts. Partly spurred by an increased, even national demand for product, designers went happily mad

Should you not
recognize them,
this pattern
labels some of its
pictures, includ-
ing "Hula",
"Leis", and
"Waikiki Beach".

with unrestrained designs and brilliant colors in sometimes dazzling combinations. The most complicated patterns were known, perhaps a little cynically, as "hash" or "chop suey" because they incorporated so many diverse pictures, usually with words labeling the subjects. More frequently, though, designers focused on certain subjects.

This golden age lasted until about the middle to late 1950s—not really a very long time. In retrospect, when the output of this period is reviewed, the huge number of prints created was astonishing—and how eye-popping some of them were. Glowing, riotous, vibrant; hula dancers, throw-net fishermen, exploding volcanoes, palm trees. Recognizable actual places: Diamond Head, Aloha Tower, Waikīkī Beach, Ala Moana Park, Nuʻuanu Pali. Actual people: Waikīkī beachboys, Hilo Hattie, Hawaiian royalty. All aspects of Hawaiian culture and artifacts: kāhili, poi pounders, fishhooks, musical instruments, feather capes. And flowers! Every possible flower: bombax, bird of paradise, angel's trumpet, night-blooming cereus, lehua, torch ginger, vanda orchids. Occasionally, everything all mixed up: pineapples and grass houses and canoes, coral and fish intermingled with flowers, footprints and crabs. And sometimes, especially on shirts made in California, single giant pictures covering the entire front or back of a shirt like an artist's canvas: a seated hula maid, a Chinese dragon, a village under the palms. (These were never tucked in; obscuring any part of the picture would be

From the same Surfriders Sportswear catalogue shown above, this separate inserted sheet shows four of the fabrics that customers could select from. At upper left is "Hawaiʻi's 'Aloha Queen,' Polynesian maiden who holds bursting torch ginger and delicate hibiscus".

The pinnacle of unique Hawaiian fabric designs was reached in the period from the late 1940s to the middle 1950s when slick, drapey rayon was popular. Understandably, it would be shirts of this special, colorful cloth that first began to attract collectors in later years. Tropical flowers were the most common motif, but scenery (both above and under water) appeared also. The pattern below covers the entire back of its shirt; next to it, at lower center, the rectangular pictures on a brown background are copied from postcards of Hawaiian subjects.

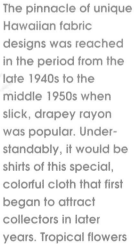

EMBROIDERED CLOTHING LABELS DATE BACK AT LEAST TO THE 1920S. SMALL IN SIZE AND MADE FOR A STRICTLY UTILITARIAN PURPOSE, NO ONE PAID MUCH ATTENTION TO THEM UNTIL COLLECTORS BEGAN TO APPRECIATE THEIR ARTISTRY AROUND 1980. TODAY, SOME MANUFACTURERS DELIBERATELY COPY OLD STYLES LIKE THESE FOR THEIR CURRENT LABELS.

A wonderful underwater fantasy of shells, fish, and the spiky leaves and flowers of the coral plant - which, despite what you see here, grows strictly on land.

Near right: Brilliant butterflies intermingle with plumeria flowers. Far right: This cotton shirt was made for the Outrigger Canoe Club in 1950 and depicts actual Waikiki beachboys, labeled with their names.

wrong!) These are the shirts that collectors, in later years, would seek above all others.

Today's observer wonders who thought up these wacky designs. There were many designers, and they sought inspiration everywhere, including in museums and private collections. Images were created from life, or from the artist's own imagination; some can be clearly traced to published photos or earlier artwork done by others. Sometimes, designers or manufacturers wanted authenticity over superficiality. At the Shaheen Company, the aim was to "create a textile design that had some meaning to it...So we tried to put in more substance into the design, and on the hangtag we'd write the story behind the design."

In the 1950s in general, patterns reached their highest use of Hawaiian subjects. Analysis of surviving shirts shows that the percentage of Hawaiian motifs rose from 57 percent in the 1940s to 67 percent in the '50s; Japanese ones fell from 18 percent to 9 percent; Chinese, other Polynesian, and batik designs made up the remainder.

The pictures are Hawaiian but the artistic style strongly suggests the work was done in Japan, the source of much rayon aloha shirt fabric.

Photo shirts were made in the 1950s, but some of the original photos used in the designs date from the 1930s. In addition to monochrome patterns like these, there are nicer shirts with pictures in color.

By the late '50s, rayon was gone. A theory first published in 1984 and widely repeated posited that the fabric disappeared because of a fire at the factory that made it. But Alfred Shaheen, who was immersed in the alohawear business at the time, states, "The idea that they quit using rayon due to a fire at DuPont is a myth. Rayon became old hat—it simply went out of style. Period." And when rayon departed, the more gaudy floral designs that had been printed on it came to be considered too garish and so were no longer fashionable, either.

The winding down of the more outrageous phase of the aloha shirt in the late '50s does not imply that the vitality of the industry—or the imagination that went into inventing patterns—diminished in any way. In a number of ways popular taste shifted from more realistic artwork, as featured on the shirts of the early '50s, to geometric, atomic-age abstractions. Aloha shirts followed this trend, which lasted through the 1960s and into the '70s.

By the late '50s, popular design taste had shifted from the realistic images formerly used in chop suey prints to more abstract, geometric patterns.

56

Another in a long line of outstanding garments styled and manufactured by Kamehameha! In this exquisite elasticized swim suit, produced in a variety of original prints—including the Matson Menu print illustrated—Kamehameha has developed a notable successor to the many earlier "firsts" already acknowledged by the nation's retail and wholesale trade.

Additional garments, handled by exclusive stores on the Mainland and in Hawaii, include tropical sportswear for all members of the family.

KAMEHAMEHA GARMENT COMPANY, LIMITED

The mainland falls for aloha shirts: the text in this 1950 advertisement in a national magazine ties its product to a popular song ("Happy Talk") from the hit Broadway show "South Pacific".

Well dressed natives (from Palm Beach to Palm Springs) are happy-talking about our new "Polynesian Print" Sportshirts—rich, washable rayon... $5.

Manhattan
THE MARK OF QUALITY SINCE 1857

In 1952, Kamehameha Garment Co. shows off its "Miss Hawai'i" elasticized bathing suit bearing the artwork of Eugene Savage (see p. 58.)

Mainland manufacturers had discovered aloha shirts in 1950, and for the next few years, in addition to the output of local manufacturers, many bigger companies sold their own "sport shirts" in the aloha vein. The increased demand helped spur creativity among fabric designers, who found themselves with a larger venue for their work. Major department stores such as Sears and J.C. Penney's retailed the fad throughout the country. (Hawai'i's first Penney's opened in 1966, so Japanese rayon shirts with the Penney's label from the '50s were only sold on the mainland, never in the islands.) While mainland manufacturers were strong competitors to

Hawai'i residents were excited to attain full citizenship with statehood in 1959, and this shirt plainly showed the wearer's pride.

Matson Lines, the main carrier of passengers be-tween Hawai'i and the west coast in the 1930s and '40s, commissioned artist Eugene Savage to paint six uniquely-interpreted murals of Hawaiian scenes in 1938. These were subsequently used on the covers of the company's dinner menus, which were saved as souvenirs by many passengers from 1948 to about 1955. Matson allowed the designs to be repro-duced on fabric, as shown here. The actual menu (entitled "Island Feast") is at top, with its cloth counterpart (which also incorpo-rates elements from other Savage menus) below.

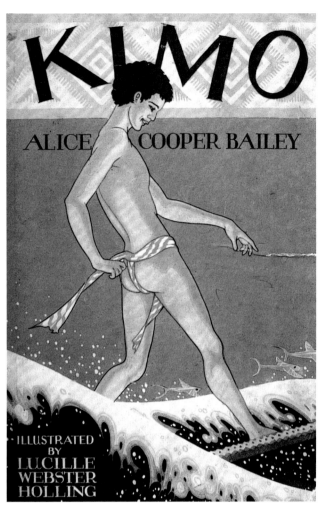

The demand for Hawaiian fabric in the 1940s and '50s kept commercial artists busy turning out patterns, and they needed constant inspiration. Sharp-eyed people can spot designs that clearly were copied from other sources. In this case, Kimo (on the cover of this 1928 children's book) was reproduced (facing the other direction) on mainland-made swim trunks manufactured by Princeton Sportswear. This fabric is known to have been on the market in 1946.

local ones, increased general demand could only help Hawai'i companies. In one promotion, Filene's of Boston claimed to have "the largest exhibit of Hawaiian material ever assembled outside the islands," and some of the merchandise was made by Kamehameha and Kahala, and transported to Boston via Pan American World Airways and American Airlines.

The United States has regularly experienced fads for Hawaiian things, and this was true for much of the 1950s, partly due to a steady barrage of news stories about Hawai'i's attempts to attain statehood. When Hawai'i finally became the 50th state in 1959, fascination with the islands blossomed. Americans became captivated at this time by an ideal of Hawai'i as not just romantic, but appealingly primitive as well—a place where people could cut loose a little. The exotic music of Martin Denny and Arthur Lyman, a mixture of jazz and other non-American elements originated and recorded in Hawai'i, was the perfect accompaniment to a trip to one of the exotic Polynesian-themed restaurants that spread during the decade. You could even play the music at home in your own tiki bar, if

you went so far as to build one in the basement (and people really did.) Small wonder, with this sort of thing going on in suburban America,

Montgomery Clift and Donna Reed smile at Frank Sinatra in the classic 1954 film "From Here to Eternity". Actors in this movie appear in a number of eye-catching shirts that were on the market at the time it was made; the best known of these is shown at right, which Clift wears during his death scene at the film's end.

that sales of alohawear—seen both as a souvenir item for tourists and as something to be worn while relaxing back at home—almost tripled during the 1950s.

Movies and television helped spread the awareness of aloha shirts. John Wayne and James Arness went comfortably native in "Big Jim McLain" (1952) as federal agents tracking Communist spies infiltrating Hawai'i. Two movies of lesser status, "Naked Paradise" and "She-Gods of Shark Reef," both filmed on location on Kaua'i in 1957, boasted onscreen costume credits for Alfred Shaheen. Far above these in dramatic content, and indeed a true film classic, is "From Here To Eternity." Aloha shirt fanciers have paid attention to it for years, but some have probably been misled by what Montgomery Clift, Frank

Don the Beachcomber, a famous South Seas-type restaurant, strictly required alohawear for all its lū'au attendees at Waikiki in the 1950s.

Sinatra, and Ernest Borgnine are wearing. The story takes place in 1941, leading up to the attack of December 7, but the shirts are contemporary to the early 1950s when the film was shot. Beautiful rayon shirts like the ones in the movie didn't actually exist when World War II began. On TV, especially in the early '50s, Hawai'i booster Arthur Godfrey was almost inescapable, for a time hosting an incredible three series at once and on the air four days a week. Godfrey loved the islands, and frequently appeared clad in an aloha shirt while playing the 'ukulele (for which he was often satirized). Hawai'i's statehood year also marked the beginning of the first regular television series set in the islands, "Hawaiian Eye," which ran until 1963. Although most of this was actually shot in Hollywood,

Beverly Noa models Alfred Shaheen's statehood com-memorative fabric in 1959. To emphasize Hawai'i's new status, she holds a star with the number 50 (Camille Shaheen-Tunberg).

Surrounded by dancers at the Polynesian Cultural Center, Elvis Presley belts out "Drums of the Islands" in th finale of his thir Hawai'i film, "Parc dise - Hawaiia Style", in 196

What to Wear

What to Wear

What to Wear IN HAWAII

What to Wear In Hawaii

Women's wear in Hawai'i enjoyed some innovative designs in the 1950s. Unique in appearance was the long-sleeved pākē muu ("Pākē" is Hawaiian for Chinese, and was used here for the dress's similarity to the Chinese cheongsam.).

performers on this show naturally had to wear appropriate Hawaiian garb.

For many years, Hawai'i guidebooks and promotional publications urged visitors to buy things (and thus support local businesses) during their stay in Hawai'i. From at least the 1920s, visitors were generally assured that they'd find the same familiar clothes for sale that they would at home, at similar prices. But when the local garment industry became substantial in the 1950s, publicity began to point out the different, unique clothing it was hoped tourists would purchase. A Hawai'i Visitors Bureau brochure of the late '50s, *What To Wear In Hawai'i*, said, "To be sure of having the right clothes, shop in Hawai'i!...*Plan now to dress the Hawaiian way.* Talented Island designers create lighthearted fashions for us, and the visitor who can resist an immediate change into them is rare indeed...The men will want to start collecting aloha shirts, which range from conservative to flamboyant. There are hundreds of patterns, so wait until you arrive before buying yours. Aloha shirts can be worn in or out, with slacks, knee-length shorts, matching Hawaiian print boxer shorts, or with a sport coat for casual dining." A 1959 Matson Lines brochure, *Clothes For Your Shipboard and Island Vacation*, advised, "A fine selection of aloha shirts

Wondering what to wear in Hawai'i? This 1950s Hawai'i Visitors Bureau brochure (shown in three versions above) will advise you to buy lots of locally-made clothing.

A bevy of Kaua'i beauties (all clad in alohawear) surrounds Lee Marvin in the 1963 film, "Donovan's Reef".

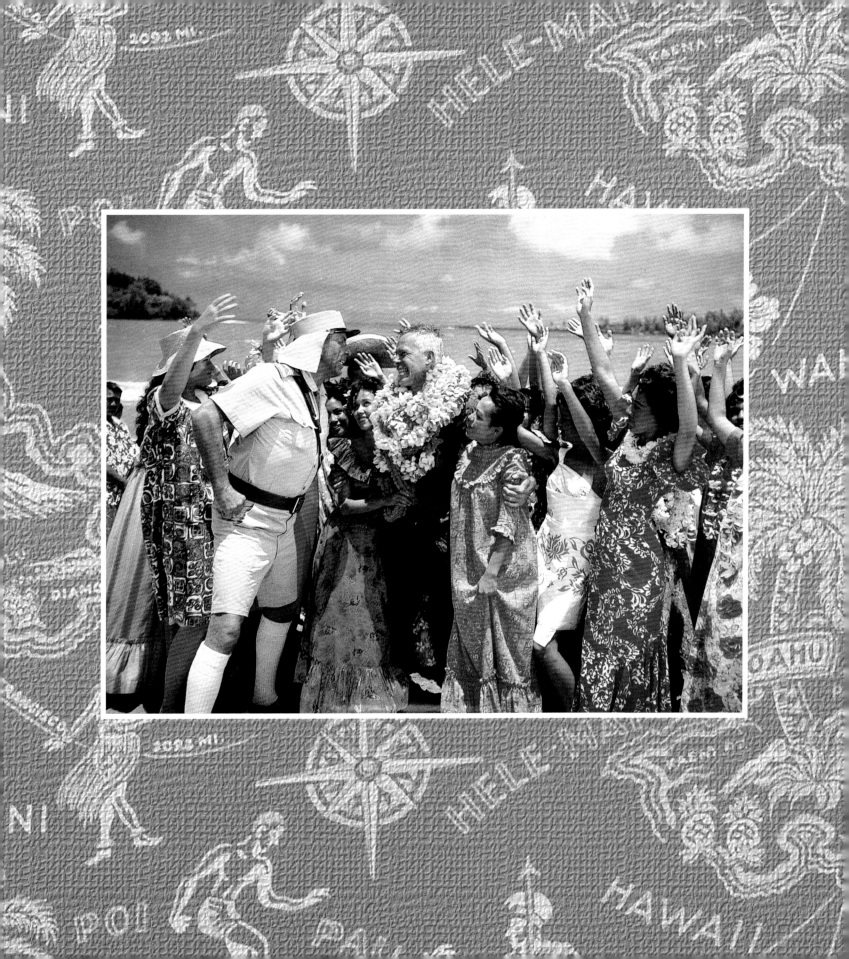

A 1956 window display at the Home Insurance Co. in downtown Honolulu promotes another local business, Hawaiian Togs, with drapes of its "Newest Exclusive Print, Kahili Ginger".

A 1952 postcard gently pokes fun at a tourist couple dressed in matching aloha outfits.

is available in Honolulu shops. Many of the designs obtainable here never reach the mainland stores."

While the basic structure of a men's shirt does not change much, women's clothing styles offer opportunities for creative cut and construction. Various women's garments, unique to Hawai'i, were already established—the loose, voluminous mu'umu'u, and the more fitted holokū, which was usually seen as a formal outfit, sometimes with a lengthy train. Between the two was a style introduced in 1949, the holomu'u. (In the '20s and '30s, women of means had holokū made to order, or would perhaps sew their own if that wasn't a possibility; these weren't usually available off the rack.) Such dresses

DRESS   3806
PRINT   B4
PRICE   7.75

SURF 'N SAND

This striking Alfred Shaheen sarong dress is an example of creative Hawaiian women's fashions in the fifties (Camille Shaheen-Tunberg).

were often made of plain silk or satin, but some used prints of flowers with no tropical connections, such as roses. As Japanese fabric became popular, and was then joined with Hawaiian designs, these were commonly used. (The vertical patterns of tropical leaves and flowers known as border prints, often appearing on rayon in the late '40s and early '50s, looked especially striking when used to make a long holokū.) In the 1950s, in addition to traditional dresses, Hawai'i-made women's wear flowered with some really innovative styles. This period saw the "pākē muu," a long dress with elongated sleeves that tapered to a sharp point. Other interesting garments: capri pants in solid colors combined with a

The classic mu'umu'u as interpreted by Shaheen in the 1950s (Camille Shaheen-Tunberg).

67

patterned top or longer tunic, blouses of different cuts, and sarong-inspired dresses that left one shoulder bare. Details were often adapted from traditional Chinese or Japanese styles. By the middle 1960s the opportunities for such specialty designs dwindled, however, and locally produced women's fashions returned to looking pretty much like those in the rest of America, except (of course) for the fabric.

A popular fad in the 1950s was matching aloha prints. Men's "cabana sets" (a shirt and boxer-style trunks of the same fabric) really took off then, although they'd been invented in the late 1930s. Dating from this period, too, were the first his-and-hers matching sets—a shirt for him and a dress or mu'umu'u for her in an identical pattern. Dressing like this was vacation fun for many couples, marking them instantly and irrevocably as tourists. Carrying the theme even further, sometimes entire family groups, including the kids (which were numerous in many families in the '50s), dressed alike. Lasting for years, the fad tapered off until by the 1990s it was rare to see the clichéd matching couple in Waikiki anymore.

A '50s family of mannequins shows how Mom, Dad, and the kids could all dress alike in Shaheen Hawaiian wear. People did it in real life then, too (Camille Shaheen-Tunberg).

Saratoga Road, Waikīkī, 1985: Judging by what they're wearing, do you think they might be tourists? (Joe Carini, Bishop Museum)

The battle for a more comfortable workplace, begun in the previous decade, continued. In 1954, some local businesses began to encourage broader acceptance of the aloha shirt. Men were asked to wear them throughout the humid summer, but were cautioned that they needed to be "clean and tucked in." One newspaper editor expressed hope that other businessmen would join in wearing local attire.

Although Honolulu's county government continued to insist that sportswear was not acceptable dress for its 5,000 men, in 1958 Hawai'i's Territorial government agreed to "permit all its male employees to wear plain, short-sleeved sport shirts of subdued colors beginning on or about June 15 and extending through the end of Aloha Week. They will be required…to wear these shirts tucked in. Aloha shirt prints will not be permitted, but it is safe to assume that a conservative design on the pockets will be generally allowed." Iolani, a local manufacturer, designed many shirts of this variety and became well-known for conservatively styled aloha shirts geared for a Hawai'i clientele.

The matching men's cabana set, by Laguna (near right) and Jantzen (facing page).

"PAU PRESS / NO MO IRON" ON THIS IOLANI LABEL MEANS LESS WORK BUT (UNFORTUNATELY) LESS COMFORT DUE TO SYNTHETIC FABRIC'S INABILITY TO BREATHE.

A tiny pair of embroidered surfers is the only Hawaiian pattern on this Reef-label shirt from the late 1950s.

As noted, in the late 1950s rayon gradually disappeared, replaced by plain cotton as well as blends of cotton and Arnel, with the promise of "permanent press" fabrics to come. These would eliminate the aggravating tendency of silk and rayon—and even cotton, to a lesser extent—to wrinkle immediately upon wearing. It would take a while for the pendulum to partly swing back to natural fibers when people discovered that wrinkle-free synthetics were also just plain uncomfortably hot. But larger changes than these were approaching in the upcoming decades, beginning with the 1960s.

Small, restrained
motifs like these,
silk-screened on this
cotton shirt, were
the type deemed
acceptable for
Hawai'i government
employees to wear
to work starting in
the late 1950s.

This Pepsi-Cola aloha shirt is from the 1950s; similar shirts with the locally-brewed Primo Beer logo were also made then. Completely different Primo shirts of the '60s and '70s are more familiar (see p. 94).

Identity Apparel and Special Editions

Identity apparel is just another name for a work uniform. But in Hawai'i, the term doesn't necessarily mean a polyester jumpsuit with a name patch on the front. Instead, it refers to a garment made of a specially-created aloha print. In some cases the pattern is not specific to the company, but in others, the design incorporates unique elements that represent that business exclusively. Often this is a small version of the company's logo, scattered around a typical aloha print.

Identity apparel became especially popular starting in the 1970s, but it existed much earlier. A shirt made of fabric bearing the Pepsi-Cola script dates from the 1950s and might have been worn by a bottling plant worker; other employees were not likely to have been so casually dressed at that time. (This particular version of the soft drink's logo was used from 1950 to 1963.) In the middle 1960s, United Airlines began attiring its flight attendants in alohawear for flights to Hawai'i; going to the mainland they wore the same uniforms as attendants in the rest of the country. By the late 1980s, with the retail market tight, the identity

Hawaiian Airlines replaced drab, military-like stewardess uniforms with sunny flower patterns in 1968.

You're only with us for 28 minutes.
We'll make every second count.

We don't have much time to impress you. So we try to make every second count. To keep the cocktails coming the way you like them. And the newspapers. And whatever else will add fun to your flight. Sure your trip is short. But Hawaiian makes it short and sweet.

HAWAIIAN AIRLINES
WE GIVE YOU A BETTER TIME.

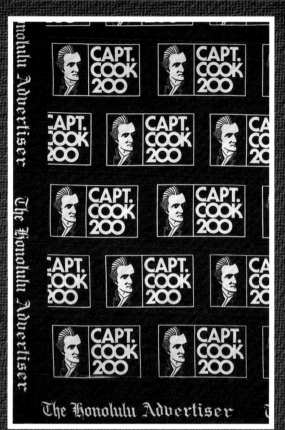

This scarf, sold by the Honolulu Advertiser, commemorated the two-hundredth anniversary of Capt. Cook's arrival in Hawai'i in 1778.

DESIGNER LOGOS BEGAN TO APPEAR PROMINENTLY ON CLOTHING IN THE LATE 1970S. BY THEN, IN HAWAI'I, SOME ALOHA SHIRTS BEARING COMPANY NAMES HAD ALREADY BEEN SOLD TO THE GENERAL PUBLIC. THEME RESTAURANTS, WHICH SPREAD IN THE 1980S AND '90S, FOUND THEY COULD DO THE SAME IN THEIR HAWAI'I LOCATIONS AS THEY ACTIVELY MERCHANDISED THEIR OWN LOGOWEAR (SEE BELOW).

apparel side of the business came to be significant (even life-sustaining) for some manufacturers.

Fabric was also created that subtly advertised companies such as United Airlines or Pan American Airways by depicting their aircraft; these examples date from around 1950 and are too early to have been worn on the job by employees. The United Airlines tie-in, at least, may have served some promotional purpose, in addition to being sold at retail. Images of Waikiki's famous Moana and Royal Hawaiian hotels showed up as well, and these probably appeared just because they formed such an integral part of the beach scene. Even better known than these hotel images were two series of famous menus used on Matson Lines' ships, which for a time were the main carriers of visitors to the Hawaiian Islands. Menus bearing well-known artwork by Frank McIntosh (used from about 1937 to 1947) and Eugene Savage (used

from about 1948 to 1955) were printed for one meal only, so travelers could save them as souvenirs. So many ended up framed in people's homes that when fabric using the same designs appeared in the 1950s, nearly everyone in Hawai'i would have been able to identify the company being indirectly advertised.

Material made just for specific events (one-time or yearly) is known as well. In some cases these designs were issued for conventions, as for the Shriners, who have held several in Waikiki. Major sporting events, school carnivals (or graduating classes), and even large family gatherings have all been commemorated by special fabric designs. Material made for political campaigns existed, too, starting around 1960. In some cases, garments of the unique cloth were intended only for specific people (workers, volunteers) while in others they might be offered for sale to raise money. Having custom shirts and dresses made for an event could add to the fun, but doing so would be extremely expensive. So nowadays this same function is filled by t-shirts, whose pictures and slogans have been a preferred mode of expression since the late '60s.

In a slightly different vein are shirts that honor events of historical importance. There are examples commemorating the Pearl Harbor attack in 1941 (although they undoubtedly date from at least the postwar period), Hawai'i's statehood in 1959, and the bicentennial of the arrival of Captain James Cook (1978).

The Hawaiian Open is an annual golf tournament. Both the shirt (above) and badge (below) use its logo, which incorporates the outline of an airplane to acknowledge the sponsorship of United Airlines in the 1970s.

marshal

Waialae C.C. Honolulu 7 Jan. 26 Feb.1

hawaiian open

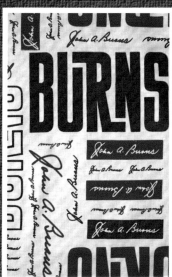

Above: William Quinn and John Burns were political adversaries in the early 1960s.

Right: Motorcycle-riding Shriners sport spiffy jumpsuits for the 1985 Aloha Week Parade (Joe Carini, Bishop Museum).

Promoting acceptance of printed aloha wear for business attire went into full swing in 1962 when the Hawaiian Fashion Guild (a professional association of manufacturers) staged "Operation Liberation." The Guild gave each man in the State House of Representatives and the Senate two aloha shirts. As a result the Senate passed a resolution urging the regular wearing of aloha attire starting on Lei Day (May 1) and continuing throughout the summer. The organization subsequently launched a campaign to institute Aloha Friday within the business community, encouraging employers to allow aloha attire to be worn to work every Friday. Aloha Friday officially commenced in 1966, and by the end of the decade the aloha shirt had become accepted in Hawai'i as business dress any day of the week. Alfred Shaheen recalled in later years how the change finally occurred: "It was really provincial in Hawai'i then; the old-timers were into formality. They weren't far from missionaries; in fact, many were descendants of the missionaries so they were still pretty strict and puritanical about things. These were the top guys in business—haoles (Caucasians)—who ran things. So it was a new breed, the younger guys who were ready for a new style."

The once-a-week casual dress custom slowly spread to the U.S. mainland via California, where some powerful businessmen of the '80s had been wearing aloha shirts since their youth in the early 1960s. The surfing fad that swept the country then had originated in California, but its roots, of course, were in Hawai'i, where some lucky mainland surfers had visited or lived; when they returned home, they took the requisite aloha shirts with them. These became associated in California with being young and hip, and wearing Hawaiian shirts in suburban high schools and colleges became a fad

Nothing too flashy about this Alfred Shaheen cotton shirt with restrained silk-screened designs (Camille Shaheen-Tunberg).

that led to a more casual style of dress overall. As Herb Kawainui Kane wrote in *Islands* magazine in 1986, "By the late 1960s, informality of dress became something of a civil right."

From the West Coast the custom of a weekly casual dress day grew in the 1990s to become what's now internationally observed as Casual Friday. Outside Hawai'i, discussion on this issue continues: does dressing informally hinder professionalism? What exactly constitutes appropriate casual attire? (especially troublesome in buttoned-down Japan) What if an employee doesn't feel comfortable in such clothes? And so on.

As already noted, alohawear is now worn every business day in Hawai'i so although the phrase Aloha Friday is still used, it's now just a pleasant way to describe the last work day before the relaxation of the weekend.

In the early '60s, a new manufacturer, Reyn's, filled the need for business shirts. Reyn McCullough had owned a men's clothing store in California before moving to Hawai'i in 1959; he joined with Ruth Spooner to design a preppy, all-cotton aloha shirt with tapered lines and a button-down, two-piece collar. McCullough carved out a niche in the local market by making a shirt dignified enough for his local customers to wear for a casual evening out, and (eventually) to the office.

During the 1960s, textile design evolved in two different directions. Many people, including tourists, continued to favor the bold, brightly-colored patterns that had long been popular. But others, especially residents, began to favor more subtle designs for business wear.

THE RESTRAINED LOOK OF AN INSIDE-OUT PRINT IS SO COMMONPLACE TODAY THAT IT'S HARD TO REALIZE WHAT A DEPARTURE THIS ORIGINALLY WAS FROM THE TYPICAL ALOHA SHIRTS THAT HAD PRECEDED IT. EVEN STRANGER WAS THE IDEA OF MANUFACTURING QUANTITIES OF CLOTHING THAT LOOKED INTENTIONALLY "WRONG" THIS WAY.

Some things never go out of style: the "subtle reverse print" of this Reyn's shirt (shown here in 1972) is still the choice for professional men at work.

Lahaina Sailor

Reminiscent of the whaling days at the turn of the century, this print captures true Hawaiiana; showing the Hawaiian State flag; Hawaii State bird, the Nene Goose; a cluster of small white flowers from the Kukui tree; and our State flower, the hibiscus.

This subtle reverse print is ideal for all Aloha occasions.

Reyn's MEN'S WEAR

Ala Moana   Kauai Surf
Kahala Mall   Kona Inn
Kahala Hilton   Royal Lahaina

The use of Hawaiian motifs decreased in favor of a wider diversity of ethnic ones, many of which were scaled down in size. Many of the newly-popular restrained designs had no Pacific or Asian attributes at all, but instead were purely American. This was true in some cases of the major innovation of the 1960s, the use of reverse prints in aloha shirts. Often called "inside out shirts," these were made with the back side of the fabric intentionally facing outward. This was popular partly because the backward cloth made a shirt look almost like it was faded instead of brand new—a well-worn favorite aloha shirt, to some young men (such as surfers), showed you were a long-term resident, not a tourist. In later years this toned-down look came to be almost a requirement for aloha shirts worn to work by professional men.

Particularly popular in the early 1960s was the "jack shirt." This was short, made to be worn untucked, and styled with the Eisenhower jacket in mind; button tabs at the shirt hem tightened the garment just below the waist. Predominantly manufactured in solid fabrics, the jack shirt with a small logo on the pocket was often worn by men who worked with the

Who says Republicans are all conservative? The Hawai'i delegation to the 1972 Republican National Convention certainly wasn't in these matching aloha print jackets (See p. 85.) (Bishop Museum).

public. (This may have been a carryover of the restrictions that the Territorial government placed on aloha shirts worn at work in the previous decade.) Many islanders remember the jack shirt as being a uniform of sorts for men who worked in hotels, as a predecessor to aloha shirts worn as uniforms for those in service industries—what has become known as identity apparel.

Identity apparel might use a generic aloha print, but frequently the pattern was unique to that company. It often incorporated the business' logo, or perhaps pictures of its headquarters building, its products, or some other relevant imagery. Such garments were not usually sold to the public, but when they were, they functioned as free advertising.

In the same way that aloha shirts once mildly shook up the concept of appropriate men's apparel, a revolution in the larger scope of men's clothing occurred in the '60s. The changes included an explosion of color, new fabrics, and some daring styles. To this, Hawai'i contributed the aloha print men's jacket, first marketed in 1967 under the First Break label by Malia. As *Honolulu* magazine stated in a stab at sounding hip, "If you are young, and dare to be bold, get with it. Take a tip from the male bird and show your true colors. The reaction is zowie. (Ask any chick.)" Within a few years the trend

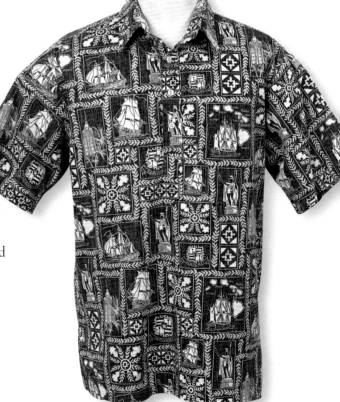

A 1990s version of the inside-out shirt, made by RJC, incorporates Hawaiian quilts, Aloha Tower, King Kamehameha, and other local favorites (University of Hawai'i's CTAHR Historic Costume Collection).

It's not enough to just sample poi at a luau; you've got to dress the part as well. These tourists enthusiastically go native at a Royal Hawaiian Hotel luau around 1965. Note that the musicians, too, are dressed in matching prints.

extended to similarly styled men's jumpsuits, which seemed more appropriate for stage performances than for everyday wear. Marketed into the middle '70s, today print jackets are an instantly recognizable moment in local fashion for those who remember when they were new.

As already stated, as the '60s progressed the old-fashioned "chop suey" prints popular until the late 1950s were abandoned and nearly discredited by the larger manufacturers in favor of cleaner and more abstract patterns. The heavy rayon they'd been printed on was out of style as well. But then there was a shift in a small but growing segment of the population that was about to rediscover these old shirts.

The 1960s saw the rise of hippies: young people who deliberately chose to live outside many of society's rules, most notably in how they looked. Men sported moustaches and beards and let their hair grow to unacceptable lengths; women rejected makeup and elaborate, sprayed hairdos. And both sexes sought secondhand clothes, not only because they were cheaper but also because they made a statement against consumerism and establishment expectations. By the early 1970s, Salvation Army and

Only at Sears...Plumeria Tapa in 100% easy care cotton, blue or brown, pants set or muumuu...Sizes 6 to 16...$18.00

Sears | For everything Hawaiian...ask for our Hawaiian Catalog or write Sears Personal Shopper, P. O. Box 3770, Honolulu, Hawaii 96815
ALA MOANA CENTER | Phone: 949-4411

Sears Hawaiian Shop in Ala Moana Center was a cornucopia of men's and women's alohawear in 1969.

Loud Jackets for a Loud Fourth of July

Goodwill outlets were joined by smaller, intentionally hip stores that sold selected old clothes. Old aloha shirts were featured goods, even on the mainland, precisely because of their outdated appearance. A 1972 article in the free Honolulu biweekly paper *Sunbums* described a jaunt through a variety of thrift shops. The writer's personal quest was to "finally get an aloha shirt that many of my friends say they got for 50 cents." After some disappointments (in one place, "the cheapest aloha shirt I saw was $4.88") he was pleased to find "a silk aloha shirt for me—for 25 cents. Well, it did have a stain..." In this period, old aloha shirts became known locally as "silkies" due to the misidentification of the slippery rayon nearly all of them were made of (although a few were of real silk.) And, as noted above, their prices began to ascend. What had been 50 cents or $1.00 gradually inched upward to an unheard-of $5.00, even at the Salvation Army (which began to put the prized old shirts aside to sell as prestige pieces).

Until this period, only a handful of pioneering aloha shirt collectors appreciated this unique Hawaiian garment both for its artistic qualities and

The updated matching alohawear couple, in 1967 (but you never would have seen them on the beach together like this in real life.) (Courtesy PacificBasin Communications)

Different trends in aloha shirts. Top left: The waist-length jack shirt, popular in the late '50s to the early '60s. Three examples of identity apparel: top right, Bishop Museum; bottom left, Building Industry Association of Hawai'i; bottom right, United Airlines/Hawaiian Open golf tournament (University of Hawai'i's CTAHR Historic Costume Collection).

In 1970, the aloha print jumpsuit had its all-too-brief moment of glory.

its fun appearance. But with the renewed stylishness of the old shirts came, first, more serious collectors who didn't just wear the shirts till they fell apart, they preserved them. Growing collector interest brought increased publicity about the shirts (in some cases spreading unfortunate misinformation, such as the assertion that aloha shirts date to the 1920s, that can never be corrected) and newly-manufactured copies that brought the same chop suey prints back into fashion. And over the following decades the once-unfashionable originals went up astronomically in value, eventually making a few lucky sellers a good deal of money. Part of the reason for the boom in high-priced old shirts came, interestingly, from Japan. Of course much of the material for the original garments had come from there, and the Japanese had long been intrigued by things Hawaiian; in the 1950s, aloha shirts had been faddish for them as well. But their astonishing boom economy in the 1980s led the Japanese to become worldwide buyers of all manner of merchandise, often with a money-is-no-object attitude. A stream of

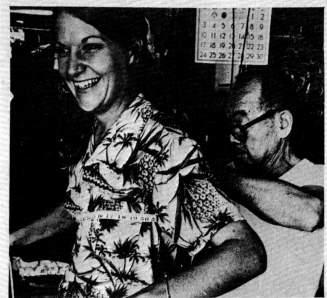

collectible Americana purchased at premium prices made its way to Japan, in turn inspiring U.S. dealers to seek out and cater to these dependable customers.

Published articles about the re-emergence of the old prints appeared in both national fashion magazines and Hawai'i publications. In "Hawai'i: Fashions As Colorful As the Islands" in *Aloha* magazine (1979), Dee Dickson wrote, "Colorful Hawaiian prints from territorial days are being used not only for men's aloha shirts but for women's blouses, jackets, dresses and shorts as well. Imprinted with island motifs—pineapples, surfers, tropical flowers, hula girls, ukuleles, steamships and coconut palms— silkies are executed in the art deco style...Today [1979] there are 130 apparel manufacturers turning out 'new' silkies, traditional mu'umu'u and aloha shirts." Vindication indeed, if any were needed, that the classic shirts of the '40s and '50s really had a lot going for them. And over 20 years after this rediscovery, patterns in the old style are still for sale.

Above left: When vintage clothes became fashionably hip, stores like the Clothes Addict supplied them; this ad is from 1976. Above right: Hard On Leather (what a name!) describes old aloha shirts in its 1972 ad: "They're called 'silkies' now but they're just as cool and comfortable as ever."

It's a shirt...it's a jacket...it's two garments in one. The Hawaiian Bush Jacket (1971) was yet another short-lived fashion direction for the aloha shirt.

For years in Hawai'i, and indeed throughout the U.S., ethnicity in many forms was denied in favor of a standardized (and idealized) American norm. But starting in the '60s and becoming strong in the '70s, people began to celebrate ethnic diversity, and some looked back with regret that their customs and languages had been dropped. In the field of alohawear, the established Asian fabrics and patterns (now including Thai silks) were joined by African kente cloth and dashiki prints, reflecting the expression of African-American pride.

Other cultures were not the only influence in the 1970s, however. In this decade, the attitude of being "local" was first being openly discussed, even celebrated; of being of Hawai'i, regardless of one's ethnicity. But more than that, people asked in earnest, what is the most unique aspect of life in Hawai'i—what is found only here, in the entire world? The answer, of course was Hawaiian culture. Retaining your ethnic background was one thing if it still thrived elsewhere; but if Hawaiian culture was not kept alive here in its home, it would be completely lost. And that threat was very real.

An updated 1990s version of the border print originally popular in the late '40s and early '50s, made by Pineapple Juice (University of Hawai'i's CTAHR Historic Costume Collection).

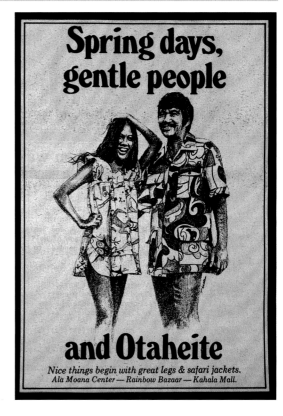

The response to this came in the form of what was termed the Hawaiian Renaissance of the 1970s. Not just acknowledging a general localness, this movement specifically honored ethnic Hawaiianness, and people began to focus on preserving what was left of it. In a process that still continues today, the '70s saw the beginning of the growth in speaking Hawaiian; the carrying on of long-distance Polynesian voyaging (the first voyages of the recreated canoe Hōkūle'a began in 1975); and a resurgence in hula, with a concurrent boom in large-scale competitions. People also worked to relearn kapa-making, revive the ancient martial art of lua, and translate historic (and ignored) writings in Hawaiian.

A craft that gained new practitioners was Hawaiian quilting. The basic technique might have been the same as elsewhere, but the patterns, developed in the 19th century, were unique to Hawai'i. The immediately recognizable graphics of the traditional Hawaiian quilt, reduced in size and repeated on material, became a major form of design inspiration from the 1970s onward.

Aloha shirts came into international consciousness in the 1980s, when nostalgia

Signs of a 1970s aloha shirt: shoulder epaulets and a zipper front.

Better living through chemistry: polyester rules in the 1970s, along with a unique belt accessory (by Iolani, above) and three-quarter length sleeves (by Kamehameha, right) (University of Hawai'i's CTAHR Historic Costume Collection).

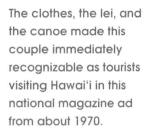

Ed Ellis didn't get a gold watch at retirement.

reigned supreme in the haute couture salons of Europe and simple patterns were considered boring. Designers "discovered" aloha prints—as though they were something new!—as Yves St. Laurent and Kenzo Okada brought out clothing lines based on Tahitian prints. Dave Rochlen of Surf Line Hawai'i noted that, in Europe, "the Art Deco movement was important and this came together with a renewed willingness to revisit...the European concept of Polynesia as Paradise." A customer in Hawai'i who wanted the prestige of a famous name could select a pricey designer aloha shirt, while locally-made versions sold for far less. Rayon, out of style since about 1960, returned to store racks. At the same time, the backlash began against "easy-care" polyester, universally worn in the previous decade—it didn't wrinkle, but people got tired of how stiff and hot it was in the warm Hawaiian climate.

A significant change gradually crept up on alohawear manufacturers by the 1990s. Their products had become expensive enough that fewer and fewer tourists bought them. Instead, the favored souvenir garment became the t-shirt, which was far cheaper to buy and more wearable once a visitor returned home. T-shirts had the additional advantage of carrying a direct, inescapable message of a trip to Hawai'i in the wording that appeared on nearly all of them ("Grandma Went To Hawai'i And All I Got Was This Lousy T-Shirt.") So manufacturers and retailers had to look toward the local market more, or to branch out in what they made or sold.

This non-flashy pattern incorporates some authentic traditional Hawaiian designs (by Holo-Holo.) (University of Hawai'i's CTAHR Historic Costume Collection)

"MELE KALIKIMAKA" ON THIS SHIRT MEANS IT'S REALLY ONLY APPROPRIATE TO WEAR AT CHRISTMAS TIME. YET THE OTHER MOTIFS ON THE SHIRT - HAWAIIAN BIRDS AND PLANTS, AND A QUILT PATTERN - ARE SO SUBTLE THAT FEW PEOPLE WOULD NOTICE THE STRICTLY SEASONAL MESSAGE. PERFECT OFFICE WEAR FOR ANY PROFESSIONAL, REGARDLESS OF THE TIME OF YEAR (BY COOKE STREET FOR LIBERTY HOUSE.) (UNIVERSITY OF HAWAI'I'S CTAHR HISTORIC COSTUME COLLECTION)

Even as this change occurred at home, however, the rest of the U.S. gained a resurgence of interest. A boom in aloha shirts—or at least something like them—found multiple mail-order catalogues offering Hawai'i's favorite attire to the nation. Some patterns were indisputably Hawaiian, such as the copies of originals from the '40s and '50s. Less authentic designs mixed in elements from various warm-weather geographic areas, lumping Caribbean, Mexican, Cuban, or South American subjects into a generic exotic world. Still other shirts dropped all this tropical stuff and depicted assorted manly things—airplanes, vintage cars, bottles of liquor, an occasional bikini-clad babe—in the same style as aloha shirts always had.

A 1980s version of the well-known Hawaiian quilt pattern (by Mamo Howell for Liberty House.) (University of Hawai'i's CTAHR Historic Costume Collection)

PARADISE ON A HANGER
THE WORLD'S FINEST ALOHA SHIRTS

VOLUME 4, NUMBER 1 SPRING/SUMMER 1990 $6.00

Paradise shirt
A 100% cotton shirt with a print of tropical flowers and plants so inviting you'll find yourself longing for the salt air. Machine wash. Regular fit.* Imported. Navy, Red.
ZC171 **$24** $29 value

Boat shirt
A brightly-colored and inarguably fun print featuring sailboats, palm trees, pineapples and a beachy backdrop. Short sleeves, reached collar. Button front. Hand wash. Relaxed fit.* 100% rayon. Imported. Boats. M-L-XL-XXL.
ZC176 **$19** $25 value

Shirts: Big color from the Big Island.

Authentic as Pele's fire, these shirts are from Reyn Spooner, Hawaii's renowned maker of Aloha shirts. They're sewn of silky imported rayon — a drapey, long-wearing poplin cloth. Handsomely...

Poke Fish. A rare back panel design recreates scenes by Hawaiian artist Dietrich Varez. Varez draws inspiration from Island legend and oral history, still works in the traditional way, printing each image by hand on hand-made rice paper. In Poke Fish, native Hawaiians spear their supper. Poke Fish. Men's Regular M-XXL.
6252-7118   69.50

4. Take a leaf from Papa Hemingway's experience and never wear a Hawaiian shirt on hunting safaris. Hemingway once wore his gaudily colored ong-of-a-kind multi-pockered, epauleted twill shirt when hunting the rare albino midget rhino, and so frightened the herd that it stampeded — and has never been seen since.

5. Loaning your H... so friends or loved on...

YOU SAY KIMONO, I SAY ALOHA
The distinctively bold Aloha Shirt traces its origins to the early 1800s, when European traders introduced colored cloth with bold designs to Hawaiian islanders. The Hawaiians altered the shirts to make short-sleeve work shirts suited to working outdoors in the tropics. The first modern garments were created in the 1930s by Ellery Chun, a tailor who made...

BLACK HIBISCUS   NAVY PINEAPPLE   GREEN T...

A vintage auto is the star on this 1990s shirt by Tori Richard, with Diamond Head in the distance (University of Hawai'i's CTAHR Historic Costume Collection).

Top: Aloha shirts again capture the American eye in mainland catalogues at the turn of the millennium. Below: Japanese tourists in Waikiki, 1985. Soon they'd favor t-shirts over aloha shirts as souvenirs (Joe Carini, Bishop Museum).

Alohawear has existed now for more than 70 years. What does it all mean? Looking back, we can see that the origins of the aloha shirt are multiethnic. European frock shirts and the Filipino barong tagalog were two of the inspirations for the concept of a loose shirt worn outside the trousers; a closer fit, with collars and buttons came from American businessmen. Japanese tailors provided kimono fabric and Chinese tailors did some of the custom tailoring in early 20th century Hawai'i. Textile designers came from a variety of ethnic backgrounds as well, and intentionally drew on the material culture of Asian and Pacific populations. Consequently, the origins of the aloha shirt draw from four diverse ethnic groups; what was created was a garment that has come to represent the varied population of Hawai'i.

In addition to specific ethnic cultural identities still prevalent in Hawai'i, there is also the concept of being local, which partly transcends but also complements these racial differences. Being local is a pan-ethnic identity, which also serves to set apart Hawai'i residents from outsiders, or visitors. While both these

Left: An exact 1990s copy of a shirt first sold around 1970 (by Go Barefoot.) Right: A very small UH logo hides in abstract patterns (by Iolani.) (University of Hawai'i's CTAHR Historic Costume Collection)

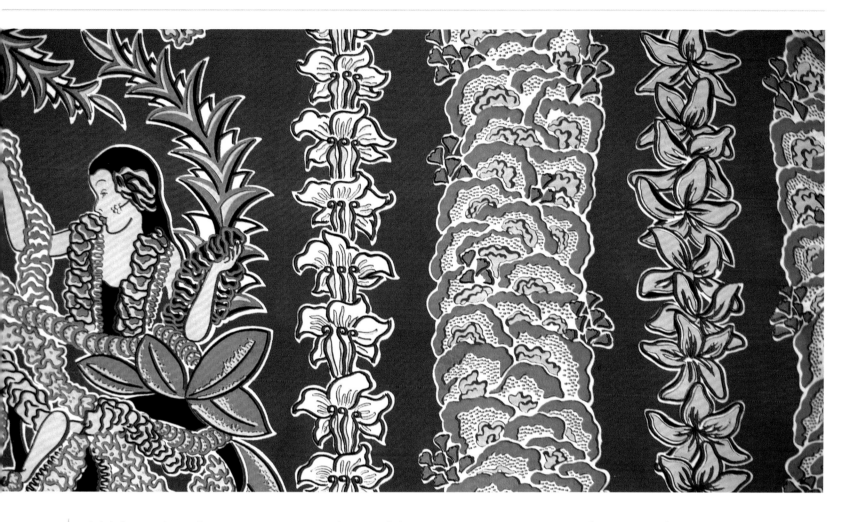

A fabric counterpart to the pleasant lei-bedecked postcard photo on the facing page. Beautiful classic aloha prints like this seem as though they might never really go out of style.

groups may dress in alohawear, variations in patterns and garment styles can also serve to visually separate them.

Ultimately, though, we see that aloha attire serves as a unifying force. As one woman described it, "Although I'm Japanese and haole [white], we have Koreans, Hawaiians, and Chinese in our family. If Auntie Reiko came to a family gathering in kimono, Auntie Grace came in a cheong sam, and Auntie Soyoung came in hanbok, we'd have a real problem! Though most of us are local and grew up here, the politics of the past can always be there under the surface. We strive for hoʻokipa [hospitable conduct] and lōkahi [harmony]. So we intentionally are careful with how we dress. Like most of us here in Hawaiʻi, we're a multiethnic family and there's no better way to show that than wearing aloha attire."

A SHAPE BECOMES AN ICON WITH UNLIMITED APPEAL

In the 21st century, aloha shirts are firmly established as an internationally recognized symbol of Hawai'i. They're so well known that now, in addition to the actual garments themselves, you can find other versions of the shirts as well.

These aren't something that anyone can actually wear. But in their way, these miniaturized copies do the same job of publicizing the Hawaiian Islands that the real things do.

There's a wonderful assortment of things made to look like this famous piece of clothing. Buyers today can choose from items as diverse as clocks, photo frames, plastic luggage tags, coasters, magnets and even mouse pads. All of these bear designs of aloha shirts, and often are even shaped like them.

The most clever adaptations of this theme are the note cards that actually open up the same way a real shirt does. Maybe it's a stretch, but you almost could imagine yourself slipping one of these on. (At least you might find yourself wishing you could find one in the same pattern in your size!) Complete with pockets and even a tiny manufacturer's label, the only thing missing is the buttons.

Maybe not everyone can wear a real aloha shirt. For those who can't, these small sized replicas - regardless of what they're made of - can be just as fun.

Above: Aloha Shirt shaped magnets - for just hanging out! At right: Chocolate covered Hawaiian Macadamia Nuts packaged in the spirit of Aloha.

Aloha Shirt shaped greeting cards for messages from the heart of aloha.

Aloha Shirt shaped clock for truly living on Hawaiian time.

PHOTO CREDITS

All images not otherwise credited are from the DeSoto Brown Collection.

Accession numbers of shirts from the University of Hawai'i's CTAHR Historic
Costume Collection:
p. 11: 96.1.13, 76.27.7
p. 16: 98.3.9
p. 21: 95.2.6, 95.2.1
p. 23: 95.2.3
p. 26: 87.12.9
p. 30: 98.14.6
p. 46: 98.14.1
p. 81: 98.3.4
p. 84: (clockwise from top left) 76.27.11, 95.6.1, 94.11.1, 96.1.24
p. 88: 94.9.2
p. 90: 96.1.16, 86.8.144
p. 92: 98.3.2, 95.2.7, 97.6.7
p. 93: no number noted
p. 94: 98.2.25, 98.17.13

This book is a collaboration of Linda B. Arthur, professor at the University of Hawai'i at Manoa, and DeSoto Brown, Hawaiiana collector and author. It is based on a text by Linda and amended by DeSoto; both provided illustrations from different sources. Information was gathered through interviews, historic publications and photos, and the collecting and examination of various surviving garments. Many of these are in the University of Hawai'i's Historic Costume Collection, of which Linda is the curator. She is also the author of *Aloha Attire: Hawaiian Dress in the 20th Century* (2000), which has served as a textbook for her classes. DeSoto is the author of *Hawai'i Recalls* (1982), *Aloha Waikīkī* (1985), *Hawai'i Goes To War* (1989) and co-author of *Coverama* (1993).